EDWARD D. ANDREWS

How Are We to Understand the
Work of and the Indwelling of
the Holy Spirit?

THE HOLY SPIRIT AND
THE CHRISTIAN

THE HOLY SPIRIT AND THE CHRISTIAN

How Are We to Understand the Work of and the Indwelling of the Holy Spirit?

Edward D. Andrews

Christian Publishing House

Cambridge, Ohio

Christian Publishing House

Professional Christian Publishing of the Good News

*THE HOLY SPIRIT AND THE CHRISTIAN
How Are We to Understand the Work of and
the Indwelling of the Holy Spirit?*

ISBN-13: 978-0692438534

ISBN-10: 069243853X

Table of Contents

CHAPTER 1 The Spirit and Christians

By Z. T. Sweeney

Updated By Edward D. Andrews

It has been aptly and truthfully said, "No importance can be attached to a religion that is not begun, carried on and completed by the Spirit of God." That the Christian is led, guided and strengthened by the Spirit cannot be denied by any Bible reader. To deny the fact that the Spirit dwells in us is to deny the Bible. However, it is asserted with equal clearness in the inspired, inerrant Word that *the Father dwells in us*. The apostle Paul wrote, "And what agreement has the temple of God with idols? For we are the temple of the living God; just as God said, '**I will dwell in them** and I will walk among them, and I will be their God, and they shall be my people.'" (2 Cor. 6:16; Lev 26:12; also similar to Jer. 32:38, Eze. 37:27) This not only says that God will dwell in us, but that he *walks in us*. It is also clearly taught that *Christ dwells in us*. Paul wrote, "So that Christ may dwell in your hearts through faith; that you, being rooted and grounded in love."–Ephesians 3:17.

Thus, we see that Scripture clearly teaches that the Father, the Son and the Holy Spirit dwell in us. The question before us is this, is there anything within Scripture that says the Holy Spirit dwells in us in a different sense from that in which the Father and the Son dwell in us? The apostle quoted from Leviticus 26:12 in our Scripture above at 2 Corinthians 6:16, where he explained what the Father meant by his words in Leviticus,

2 Corinthians 6:16 Updated American Standard Version (UASV)	Leviticus 26:12 Updated American Standard Version (UASV)
16 And what agreement has the temple of God with idols? For we are the temple of the living God; just as God said,	12 And I will also walk among you and be your God, and you shall be my people.
"I will dwell in them and I will walk among them, and I will be their God, and they shall be my people.	

The Greek word *enoikeso* literally means, "I shall indwell" *en autois* "in them." We learn from Paul's quote of Leviticus 26:12 that God had promised to be in communion with Israel. However, there is nothing in Leviticus 26:12 to show God's personal "indwelling" in any one person.

2

How does Christ dwell in us? Ephesians 3:17 quoted above says, "Christ may dwell in your hearts through faith;" the Greek literally reading *ho pisteos*, "the faith" or *the gospel*. How does the Spirit dwell in us? Paul asks the Galatians, "Did you receive the Spirit by works of the law or by the hearing of faith?" In other words, 'Did you receive the Spirit by works of the law or by the hearing of the gospel?' The above Scriptures clearly teach that when the words, thoughts and Spirit of God are controlling in our lives, *God dwells in us*; that when the gospel controls us, *Christ dwells in us*; that when we receive the gospel by the hearing of faith, *the Spirit dwells in us*.

Now, what reason has any man for declaring that the Spirit dwells in us in any other way, unless he can point to an explicit declaration of God's word defining and explaining that other way? This cannot be done, for there is no such passage. However, some might argue, "I do not have to depend upon the Word. I know it by my own consciousness." It is a principle as old as metaphysics that consciousness does not take cognizance of causes, but of effects. You may be conscious of an effect within you, but you cannot be conscious of the cause that produced the effect. Suppose you are lying asleep on the ground; a severe pain suddenly awakens you in your lower limb; consciousness tells you that you are suffering pain, but it does not tell you what produced that pain. This must be decided by *reason* or *faith*. If you find a thorn in the grass where your limb was resting, *reason* says the thorn *stuck you*. On the other hand, if you find a bumblebee mashed in the grass, *reason* will say the insect *stung you*; or, if someone near you says, a boy with a pin in his hand ran away from you, *faith* will say the boy *stuck you*. However, in either case reason or faith decided the cause of your pain. Now, when a man says, "I am conscious of the presence of the Holy Spirit within me," he simply means, "I am conscious of a *feeling* within me which I *have been taught* was caused by the Holy Spirit." If the man has been taught wrong, he assigns a *wrong cause* for the feeling. What is the feeling usually assigned for the presence of the Holy Spirit's personal indwelling? It is a feeling of joy, peace and love. However, cannot such feeling be excited by other causes?

We know there are dozens of causes that will produce such feelings. In the absence of clear testimony, what right has any one to attribute such feeling to the personal presence of the Holy Spirit? A man is found murdered. The testimony shows that any one of a dozen men could have killed him. Is there an intelligent jury in the land that would convict any one of the men of being the murderer? What would you think of a jury that would render such a verdict?

"Well," says one, "what of the great numbers who pray for a 'Pentecostal revival'? Are they all wrong?" Not wrong in what they *want*, but wrong in *what they call it*. All that those people desire, is to be filled with a *genuine revival of religious enthusiasm*. Their mistake is in calling it a "Pentecostal shower." A Pentecostal shower would lead every preacher under its influence to say, with the apostle Peter, to inquiring sinners, "Repent and be baptized every one of you in the name of Jesus Christ for the forgiveness of your sins ..." This is what they are careful *not to say*. It is clear evidence that the Spirit, which guided Peter, is not guiding them. I assert it to be a fact that the Spirit acting through the word of God as clearly accomplishes everything that is claimed to be affected by a personal indwelling of the Spirit.

I do not wish to rest content with asserting that statement, but I wish to prove it. What are the things that might be accomplished by a direct personal indwelling of the Spirit in us?

1. The Holy Spirit might give us faith.

5

This is accomplished through the Word of God.

Romans 10:17 Updated American Standard Version (UASV)

[17] So faith comes from hearing, and hearing through the word of Christ.

      2. The Holy Spirit might enable us to enjoy a new birth.

This is accomplished through the Word of God.

1 Peter 1:23 Updated American Standard Version (UASV)

[23] having been born again, not of perishable seed but of imperishable, through the living and enduring word of God.

      3. The Holy Spirit might give us light.

This is accomplished through the Word of God.

Psalm 119:130 Updated American Standard Version (UASV)

[130] The unfolding of your words gives light; it gives understanding to the simple.

      4. The Holy Spirit might give us wisdom.

This is accomplished through the Word of God.

2 Timothy 3:14-15 Updated American Standard Version (UASV)

[14] You, however, continue in the things you have learned and were persuaded to believe, knowing from whom you have learned them, [15] and that from infancy[1] you have known the sacred writings, which are able to make you wise for salvation through trust[2] in Christ Jesus.

This is accomplished through the Word of God.

Psalm 19:7 Updated American Standard Version (UASV)

[7] The law of Jehovah is perfect,
   restoring the soul;
the testimony of Jehovah is sure,
   making wise the simple

   5. The Holy Spirit might convert us.

This is accomplished through the Word of God.

---

[1] *Brephos* is "the period of time when one is very young—'childhood (probably implying a time when a child is still nursing), infancy." – GELNTBSD

[2] *Pisteuo* is "to believe to the extent of complete trust and reliance—'to believe in, to have confidence in, to have faith in, to trust, faith, trust.' – GELNTBSD

Psalm 19:7 Updated American Standard Version (UASV)

⁷ The law of Jehovah is perfect, restoring the soul ...

    6. The Holy Spirit might open our eyes.

This is accomplished through the Word of God.

Psalm 19:8 Updated American Standard Version (UASV)

⁸ The precepts of Jehovah are right,
    rejoicing the heart;
the commandment of Jehovah is pure,
    enlightening the eyes.

    7. The Holy Spirit might give us understanding.

This is accomplished through the Word of God.

Psalm 119:104 Updated American Standard Version (UASV)

¹⁰⁴ From your precepts I get understanding; therefore I hate every false way.

    8. The Holy Spirit might preserve or give us life, i.e., quicken us.

This is accomplished through the Word of God.

Psalm 119:50 Updated American Standard Version (UASV)

[50] This is my comfort in my affliction,
that your word has preserved me alive.[3]

9. The Holy Spirit might save us.

This is accomplished through the Word of God.

James 1:21 Updated American Standard Version (UASV)

[21] Therefore, putting aside all filthiness and abundance of wickedness, and receive with meekness the implanted word, which is able to save your souls.[4]

10. The Holy Spirit might sanctify us.

This is accomplished through the Word of God.

John 17:17 Updated American Standard Version (UASV)

[17] Sanctify them in the truth; your word is truth.

11. The Holy Spirit might purify us.

---

[3] Older translations read, *quickened me*

[4] Or "is able to save *you*"

This is accomplished through the Word of God.

"Seeing ye have purified your souls in your obedience to *the truth*

1 Peter 1:22 Updated American Standard Version (UASV)

[22] The souls of you having been purified by obedience to the truth, for an unhypocritical love of the brothers, intensely love one another from the heart,[5]

12. The Holy Spirit might cleanse us.

This is accomplished through the Word of God.

John 15:3 Updated American Standard Version (UASV)

[3] Already ye are clean because of the word which I have spoken unto you.

13. The Holy Spirit might make us free from sin.

This is accomplished through the Word of God.

Romans 6:17-18 Updated American Standard Version (ASV)

---

[5] Two early mss read *a clean heart*

¹⁷ But thanks be to God that you were slaves of sin, but you became obedient from the heart to that form of teaching to which you were committed, ¹⁸ and having been freed from sin, you became slaves of righteousness.

> 14. The Holy Spirit might impart a divine nature.

This is accomplished through the Word of God.

2 Peter 1:4 Updated American Standard Version (UASV)

⁴ By which he has granted to us his precious and very great promises, so that through them you may become partakers of the divine nature, having escaped from the corruption that is in the world because of sinful desire.

> 15. The Holy Spirit might fit us for glory.

This is accomplished through the Word of God.

Acts 20:32 Updated American Standard Version (UASV)

³² And now I commend you to God and to the word of his grace, which is able to build you up and to give you the inheritance among all those who are sanctified.

16. The Holy Spirit might strengthen us.

This is accomplished through the Word of God.

Psalm 119:28 Updated American Standard Version (ASV)

28 My soul weeps[6] because of grief;
strengthen me according to your word!

In the above cases, we have covered all the conceivable things a direct indwelling Spirit could do for one, and have shown that all these things the Spirit does through the word of God. It is not claimed that a direct indwelling of the Spirit makes any new revelations, adds any new reasons or offers any new motives than are found in the word of God. Of what use, then, would a direct indwelling Spirit be? God makes nothing in vain. We are therefore, necessarily, led to the conclusion that, in dealing with his children today, God deals with them in the same psychological way that he deals with men in inducing them to become children. This conclusion is strengthened by the utter absence of any test by which we could know the Spirit dwells in us, if such were the case.

---

[6] Lit *drops*

What the Spirit Does for the Christian

1. *The Holy Spirit is active in our birth.*

John 3:5 Updated American Standard Version (ASV)

⁵ Jesus answered, "Truly, truly I say to you, unless someone is born from water and spirit, he is not able to enter into the kingdom of God.

Here is a distinct statement of a radical change, so radical as to be likened to a new birth in order that we may enter the kingdom of God. What is it that is born? Christ says, "A man." However, what is a man? We regard a man as having a mind, a heart and a body. There is no perfect man where any of these elements is lacking. If, therefore, a man is born again, he must be born in mind, in heart, in body. How is this birth accomplished? Let us see what the Word says,

John 1:12-13 Updated American Standard Version (ASV)

¹² On the other hand, as many as received him, he gave authority to them to become children of God, to the *ones* trusting in his

name; **13** who were born, not of blood,[7] nor of the will of the flesh, nor of the will of man, but of God.

God gives all things—sometimes directly, sometimes through an agent. The Holy Spirit is the agent, i.e., "Born of water and the Spirit." However, an agent often works through an instrument. What is the instrument? It is the Word of God. "The souls of you having been purified by obedience to the truth, for an unhypocritical love of the brothers, intensely love one another from the heart, having been born again, not of perishable seed but of imperishable, **through the living and enduring word of God**." (1 Pet. 1:22, 23).

How can the word of God accomplish the new birth?

Paul tells us, "**All Scripture is inspired by God** and profitable for teaching, for reproof, for correction, for training in righteousness; so that the man of God may be fully competent, equipped for every good work." (2 Tim. 3:16-17) The apostle Peter tells us, "For no prophecy

---

[7] Literally "bloods." This is the only place in the NT that you will find the plural form of blood. It possible that it could refer either to hereditary (that is, blood from one's father and mother) or to the OT blood sacrifice. Neither is necessary for birth into the family of God.

was ever produced by the will of man, but **men carried along by the Holy Spirit** spoke from God." (2 Pet 1:21) The apostle Paul tells us, "For **the word of God is living and active** and sharper than any two-edged sword, and piercing as far as the division of soul and spirit, of both joints and marrow, and able to judge the thoughts and intentions of the heart." (Hebrews 4:12) The Word of God is inspired, literally God-breathed; as the Bible authors were carried along by Holy Spirit, meaning the words are is living and active. Let us listen in as New Testament Bible scholar Thomas D. Lea writes about Hebrews 4;12,

> This vivid expression of the power of God's message provides the explanation for the strong warning of verse 11. Because God's message is alive, active, sharp, and discerning, those who listen to God's message can enter his rest. Two questions are important in this verse. First, what is **the word of God?** Second, what does this passage say about it?

> Although the Bible sometimes refers to Christ as God's Word (John 1:14), the reference here is not speaking of Jesus Christ. Here we have a general reference to God's message to human

beings. In the past God had spoken to human beings through dreams, angelic appearances, and miracles. He still can use those methods today, but our primary contact with God is through his written Word, the Bible. God's Word will include any method God uses to communicate with human beings.

This verse contains four statements about God's Word. First, it is **living.** God is a **living** God (Heb. 3:12). His message is dynamic and productive. It causes things to happen. It drives home warnings to the disobedient and promises to the believer. Second, God's Word is **active,** an emphasis virtually identical in meaning with the term **living.** God's Word is not something you passively hear and then ignore. It actively works in our lives, changes us, and sends us into action for God.

Third, God's Word penetrates the **soul and spirit.** To the Hebrew people, the body was a unity. We should not think of dividing the soul from the spirit. God's message is capable of penetrating the impenetrable. It can divide what is indivisible. Fourth, God's message is discerning. **It judges the thoughts and attitudes of the heart.** It passes judgment on our feelings and our thoughts. What we regard as secret and hidden, God brought out for inspection by the discerning power of his Word. (Lea, Holman New Testament Commentary: Vol. 10, Hebrews, James 1999, 72)

George Washington put his spirit into the sentence, "United we stand, divided we fall." As long as the American people are true to the above words, the spirit of George Washington will live in them. However, make the same words read, "Divided we stand, united we fall," and the spirit of Washington is removed from them. The only way to take the Spirit of God from the word of God is to add to, take from or transpose the Word so it will not say what the Spirit *said in it*.

"Well," says one, "if we are born of the Spirit operating through the Word, must we not understand all the Word in order that we may be born again?" No, the apostle limits the part of the Word we must understand in verse 25 of this same chapter, "This word is the good news that was preached to you." Let us now endeavor to learn how the gospel, good news, produces this change. How is the mind born again! In order to learn this we must understand what is the normal condition of the mind of those who are not reborn spiritually and not repentant (unregenerate). In general, we may say it is in a state of *unbelief*. Now, the proclamation of the great facts of the death, burial and resurrection of Christ according to the Scriptures will break up that condition of unbelief and produce a conviction of the truth of the gospel. When the mind is changed from a state of unbelief to one of hearty belief, the birth of the mind is complete.

However, the mind is only a part of man. The heart must be born again. What is the normal state of the unregenerate heart? It is one of either *indifference* or *hatred*. The latter is the former fully ripened. It is said that Voltaire carried a seal ring upon which were engraved the words, "Crush the wretch," and every time he sealed a letter he impressed his spirit of hatred upon that letter. Now, the gospel sets forth the love of God in Christ and the loveliness of Christ's sacrifice for us in such a manner as to change the indifferent or malignant heart into one of supreme love to Christ. When the heart has thus been changed from hatred to love, it is born again.

However, man has also a body, and upon this spirit cannot act. If the body is to be born again, some element must be used that can act upon the body. Hence our Savior says, "born of water and the Spirit," because water can act upon the body. Now, the only use of water in the new birth is in the act of baptism. All scholars of note in the religious world agree that Christ's use of water in the new birth has reference to baptism. Paul also speaks of "having our hearts sprinkled clean from an evil conscience and our bodies washed with pure water." (Heb. 10:22) Thus, with mind and heart changed by the Spirit through the gospel, and the body solemnly consecrated to God in baptism, the entire man is born again. This is all accomplished by the Spirit of God working *in and through the gospel*.

2. Another work of the Spirit is to *"bear witness with our spirit that we are children of God, and if children, then heirs"* (Rom. 8:16). It does not say, "bear witness *to* our spirit," but "*with* our spirit." Many people gauge the witness of the Spirit by feelings within themselves. If they feel good, it is evidence to them of the Spirit's testimony, but they frequently feel bad also; whose testimony is that? The testimony of the Spirit should be clear testimony, and not fluctuating; it

should be in words, and not in feelings. Feelings, impressions and emotions come and go as the waves of the sea, but words remain forever the same. "Heaven and earth shall pass away, but my word shall not pass away," said the Lord. The idea of the conscious testimony of the Spirit is not sustained by either the Word of God or a correct psychology. It is the testimony of metaphysicians, from Sir William Hamilton down to the writer, that consciousness does not take cognizance of causes, but effects. Feelings are effects and not causes. Consciousness tells us when we feel good or bad, but it does not tell us what makes us feel good or bad. When a man has been taught that a certain feeling in the heart is produced by a certain agency, his faith and reason may decide that that agency produced the feeling, but consciousness has nothing whatever to do with *the cause* of the feeling. Likewise, a certain feeling in the heart may be attributed to the Spirit because one has been taught that the Spirit will produce such a feeling, but consciousness cannot trace that feeling to the Spirit himself. A man should feel right because he knows he is right, and not know he is right because he feels right.

In deciding whether we be children of God, we have two witnesses: first, the Spirit himself, and, second, our spirit. The Spirit testifies as to who is a child of God; our spirits testify as to what we are. If our spirits testify that we are the character, which the Spirit says belongs to a child of God, then we have the testimony of the Spirit himself bearing witness with our spirits that we are children of God. The testimony of the Spirit, in the nature of the case, must be general. He testifies that whosoever believes in Christ, repents of his sins, and is baptized into him, is a child of God. This is the whole of his testimony. Your spirit, likewise, must bear witness to your position on all of these points.

No one but your own spirit can testify that you believe in Christ; you may profess to, and the whole world may believe that you do, but your own spirit knows that you are a hypocrite in making the profession. Likewise, no one can testify but your own spirit that you have repented; you may make professions of repentance, and the world may believe you thoroughly sincere, but your own spirit may tell you that your profession is false. In a similar manner, no one but your own spirit can testify that you have been baptized; your father and mother may say so, the church record may so testify, and yet it is possible for them to be mistaken. To be certain you are a child of God you must have the testimony of your own spirit that you believe, that you have repented and that you have been baptized. If, in the judgment day, God should ask such people, "Have you obeyed me in the act of Christian baptism?" they would not have the testimony of their spirit that they had so obeyed; they would have to fall back upon the church record or that of their father and mother. Others may be satisfied with such testimony, but, as for myself, if I did not have the testimony of my own spirit that I had obeyed the Lord in Christian baptism, I would obtain that testimony before the going down of the sun.

"Well," says one "is that all the witness of the Spirit mentioned by the apostle?" Yes, that is all; absolutely and unqualifiedly all. What more can you desire? "Well," says another, "I want something more than the mere word; I want to be saved like the thief on the cross." How do you know that the thief on the cross was saved? "Oh, the Bible says he was." True, but that is the testimony of the "mere word;" so you have as much testimony to your own salvation as you have for the salvation of the thief on the cross, and it would be impossible for you to have any more. Suppose the Lord were to come down and take you up bodily and set you down before his throne in heaven, and, in the presence of all the angels and archangels, say to you: "My child, your sins are all forgiven." "Now," says one, "that would be testimony indeed." Yes, it would be testimony, but no more testimony than you have in the word of God now; you would then have only the testimony of the "mere word" of God that you were forgiven. All such criticisms arise out of infidelity as to the truthfulness of God's word.

3.   *The Spirit make intercession for us*. This is not a work done neither in us nor upon us, but is something done for us before the throne of God. We cannot dogmatize as to *how* the Spirit maketh intercession, but Paul says he does it "*according to the will of God*." This is a fact that appeals to *our faith* and not to our Christian *experience*. It "cannot be uttered." We can rest upon it and draw comfort from it as a child draws strength from its mother's breast. We can also draw comfort from the fact that Christ "always lives to make intercession" us, though we have no knowledge as to *how* he does it.

4.   Another work of the Spirit is to "*change us from glory to glory*." "But we all, with unveiled face, reflecting as a mirror the glory of the Lord, are transformed into the same image from glory to glory, even as from the

Lord the Spirit." (2 Cor. 3:18) The figure used here by the apostle is taken from the process of mirror-making among the ancients. They had not the glass mirrors of our day, but a mirror of highly polished metal. A piece of coarse metal would be placed upon a stone and the workmen would begin to polish it. At first, it made no reflection at all, but when polished for a while would give a distorted and perverted reflection; but in the process of polishing, that reflection would grow clearer and clearer, when finally a man could behold his face in it perfectly reflected. And so, the same holds true with us. When taken into the great spiritual laboratory of Christianity we are blocks in the rough, but in the polishing process of the church and spiritual surroundings we begin to reflect the image of our Master, and when we have completed the work, we reflect him as perfectly as an imperfect human being can. Take, for illustration, the brothers Peter and John. At first they were called Boanerges, sons of thunder; they wanted to call down fire from heaven to destroy men who differed from them; but in the great laboratory of the Christian life they grew more and more Christlike, transformed by the Spirit of God, until at last we see the old apostle John at Ephesus, beautified and ennobled, sitting in his chair and lifting up trembling hands, and saying to the young disciples: "Little children, love one another, for love is of God." We see the transforming power of the spiritual atmosphere of the church and the Christian life upon human nature. Christian, with this illustration before you, how can you excuse yourself for keeping out of the spiritual atmosphere of God, for staying away from the communion and the spiritual convocation of God's people? Is it a burden and a duty to attend the house of God, or is it a pleasure gladly and joyfully anticipated? When you rise on the Lord's Day morning, do you say, "Must I go to church today?" or do you say,

"You may sing of the beauty of mountain and dale, The water of streamlet and the flowers of the Vale, But the place most delightful this earth can afford, Is the place of devotion, the house of the Lord"?

5. The last work of the Spirit, which the Word of God mentions, is "giving life to our mortal bodies." "If the Spirit of him who raised Jesus from the dead dwells in you, he who raised Christ Jesus from the dead will also give life to your mortal bodies through his Spirit who dwells in you." (Rom. 8:11). This Spirit, which has ever been with us,

25

watching over us, will never leave us until he raises our bodies from the dead and fashions our vile bodies like unto the glorious body of our Lord. It matters much where we now live; it matters little where and how we die. Our bodies may be buried in the unfathomed caves of ocean; they may lie upon some mountain-peak or be placed in a crowded cemetery of some great city. No stone may mark our resting-place, no friend may be able to find the spot and place a flower of love upon it; but the infinite Spirit of God knows that abiding-place, and from our ashes, he will give life to our bodies and present us faultless before the throne of God.

CHAPTER 2 The Work of the Holy Spirit

Edward D. Andrews

Before we begin unraveling one of the touchiest topics in religious circles, it might be best if we borrow the story from Dr. Robert Stein's book, *A Basic Guide to Interpreting the Bible*:

> Tuesday night arrived. Dan and Charlene had invited several of their neighbors to a Bible study, and now they were wondering if anyone would come. Several people had agreed to come, but others had not committed themselves. At 8:00 P.M., beyond all their wildest hopes, everyone who had been invited arrived. After some introductions and neighborhood chit-chat, they all sat down in the living room. Dan explained that he and his wife would like to read through a book of the Bible and discuss the material with the group. He suggested that the book be a Gospel, and, since Mark was the shortest, he recommended it. Everyone agreed, although several said a bit nervously that they really did not know much about the Bible. Dan

reassured them that this was all right, for no one present was a "theologian," and they would work together in trying to understand the Bible.

They then went around the room reading Mark 1:1–15 verse by verse. Because of some of the different translations used (the New International Version, the Revised Standard Version, the King James Version, and the Living Bible), Dan sought to reassure all present that although the wording of the various translations might be different, they all meant the same thing. After they finished reading the passage, each person was to think of a brief summary to describe what the passage meant. After thinking for a few minutes, they began to share their thoughts.

Sally was the first to speak. "What this passage means to me is that everyone needs to be baptized, and I believe that it should be by immersion." John responded, "That's not what I think it means. I think it means that everyone needs to be baptized by the Holy Spirit." Ralph said somewhat timidly, "I am not exactly sure what I should be doing. Should I try to understand what Jesus and John the Baptist meant, or what the passage means to me?" Dan told him that what was important was what the passage meant to him. Encouraged by this, Ralph replied, "Well, what it means to me is that when you really want to meet God you need to go out in the wilderness just as John the Baptist and Jesus did. Life is too busy and hectic. You have to get away and commune with nature. I have a friend who says that to experience God you have to go out in the woods and get in tune with the rocks."

It was Cory who brought the discussion to an abrupt halt. "The Holy Spirit has shown me," he said, "that this passage means that when a person is baptized in the name of Jesus the Holy Spirit will descend upon him like a dove. This is what is called the baptism of the Spirit." Jan replied meekly, "I don't think that's what the meaning is." Cory, however, reassured her that since the Holy Spirit had given him that meaning it must be correct. Jan did not respond to Cory, but it was obvious she did not agree with what he had said. Dan was uncomfortable about the way things were going and sought to resolve the situation. So he said, "Maybe what we are experiencing is an indication of the richness of the Bible. It can mean so many things!"

But does a text of the Bible mean many things? Can a text mean different, even contradictory things? Is there any control over the meaning of biblical texts? Is interpretation controlled by means of individual revelation given by the Holy Spirit? Do the words and grammar control the meaning of the text? If so, what text are we talking about? Is it a particular English translation such as the King James Version or the New International Version? Why not the New Revised Standard Version or the Living Bible? Or why not a German translation such as the Luther Bible? Or should it be the Greek, Hebrew, and Aramaic texts that best reflect what the original authors, such as Isaiah, Paul, and Luke, wrote? And what about the original authors? How are they related to the meaning of the text?

It is obvious that we cannot read the Bible for long before the question arises as to what the Bible "means" and who or what determines that meaning. Neither can we read the Bible without possessing some purpose in reading. In other words, using more technical terminology, everyone who reads the Bible does so with a "hermeneutical" theory in mind. The issue is not whether one has such a theory but whether one's "hermeneutics" is clear or unclear, adequate or inadequate, correct or incorrect.

2 Corinthians 4:3-4 English Standard Version (ESV)

³ And even if our gospel **is veiled**, it is **veiled** to those who are **perishing**. ⁴ In their case **the god** of this world has **blinded the minds of the unbelievers**,⁸ to keep them from

---

⁸ By **unbelievers** Paul has in view non-Christians (1 Cor. 6:6; 7:12–15; 10:27; 14:22–24). First, the unbelievers of verse 4 are a subset of those who are perishing in verse 3. In other words, the two are the same. Second, the unbelievers are not persons, who have never heard the truth. No, rather, they are persons who have heard the truth, and have rejected it as foolish rubble. This is how this writer is using the term "unbeliever" as well. Technically, how could one ever truly be an unbeliever if

31

seeing the light of the gospel of the glory of Christ, who is the image of God.

2 Corinthians 3:12-18 English Standard Version (ESV)

[12] Since we have such a hope, we are very bold, [13] not like Moses, who would put a veil over his face so that the Israelites might not gaze at the outcome of what was being brought to an end. [14] But **their minds were <u>hardened</u>**. For to this day, when they read the old covenant, that same **veil remains unlifted**, because only **through Christ is it taken away**. [15] Yes, to this day whenever Moses is read a **veil lies over their <u>hearts</u>**. [16] But **<u>when one turns</u>** to the Lord, the **veil is removed**. [17] Now the Lord is the Spirit, and where the Spirit of the Lord is, there is freedom. [18] And we all, with unveiled face, beholding the glory of the Lord, are being transformed into the same image from one degree of glory to another. For this comes from the Lord who is the Spirit.

---

they had never heard and understood the truth, to say they did not believe the truth? Therefore, to be an unbeliever, one needs to hear the truth, understand the truth, and reject that truth (i.e., not believing the truth is just that, the truth).

Let us start by looking at an example of blind minds within Scripture. This was not a case of physical blindness, but mental blindness. There was a Syrian military force coming after Elisha, and God **blinded them <u>mentally</u>**. If it had been physical blindness, then each of them would have to have been led by hand. However, what does the account say?

2 Kings 6:18-20 American Standard Version (ASV)

¹⁸ And when they came down to him, Elisha prayed to Jehovah, and said, Please strike this people with blindness. And he struck them with blindness according to the word of Elisha. ¹⁹ And Elisha said to them, This is not the way, neither is this the city: follow me, and I will bring you to the man whom you seek. And he led them to Samaria. ²⁰ And it came to pass, when they were come into Samaria, that Elisha said, Jehovah, open the eyes of these men, that they may see. And Jehovah opened their eyes, and they saw; and, behold, they were in the midst of Samaria.

Are we to believe that one man led the entire Syrian military force to Samaria? If they were physically blind, they would have to have all held hands. Were the Syrian military forces not able physically to see the images that were before them? No, rather, it was more of an inability to understand them. This must have been some form of mental blindness, where we see everything that everyone else sees, but something just does not register. Another example can be found in the account about the men of Sodom. When they were blinded, they did not become distressed, running into each other.

Definitely, Paul is speaking of people, who are not receptive to truth, because their heart is hardened to it, callused, unfeeling. They are not responding, because their figurative heart is opposed. It is as though, God handed them over to Satan, to be mentally blinded from the truth, not because he disliked them per se, but because they had closed their hearts and minds to the Gospel. Thus, no manner of argumentation is likely to bring them back to their senses.

HOWEVER, at one time Saul (Paul) was one of these. Until he met the risen Jesus on the road to Damascus, he was mentally blind to the truth. He was well aware of what the coming Messiah was to do, but Jesus did none of these things, because it was not time. Thus, Paul was blinded by his love for the Law, Jewish tradition and history. So much so, he was unable to grasp the Gospel. Not to mention, he lived during the days of Jesus ministry, studied under Gamaliel, who was likely there in the area. He could have even been there when Jesus was amazing the Jewish religious leaders, at the age of twelve. Therefore, Saul (Paul) needed a real wake up call, to get through the veil that blinded him.

Hence, a mentally blind person sees the same information as another, but the truth cannot or will not get down into their heart. I have had the privilege of talking to dozens of small groups of unbelievers, ranging from four people to ten people in my life. I saw this in action. As I spoke to these groups, inevitably, I would see the light going off in the eyes of some (they would be shaking their heads in agreement as I spoke), but others having a cynical look, a doubting look (they would be shaking their heads in disgust or disapproval), and they eventually walked away. This is not saying that the unbeliever cannot understand the Bible; it is simply that they see no significance in it, as it is foolishness to them.

1 Corinthians 2:14 The Lexham English Bible (LEB)

[14] But the natural man <u>does not accept</u> the things of the Spirit of God, for <u>they are foolishness</u> to him, and <u>he is **not able to**</u>

understand[9] them, because they are spiritually discerned.

Hundreds of millions of Christians use this verse as support that without the "Holy Spirit," we can fully understand God's Word. They would argue that without the "Spirit" the Bible is nothing more than foolish nonsense to the reader. What we need to do before, arriving at the correct meaning of what Paul meant, is grasp what he meant by his use of the word "understand," as to what is 'foolish.' In short, "the things of the Spirit of God" are the "Spirit" inspired Word of God. The natural man sees the inspired Word of God as foolish, and "he is not able to understand them."

Paul wrote, "But the natural man does not accept the things of the Spirit of God, for they are foolishness to him." What did Paul mean by this statement? Did he mean that if the Bible reader did not have the "Spirit" helping him, he would not be able to grasp the correct meaning

---

[9] "The Greek word *ginosko* ("to understand") does not mean comprehend intellectually; it means know by experience. The unsaved obviously do not experience God's Word because they do not welcome it. Only the regenerate have the capacity to welcome and experience the Scriptures, by means of the Holy Spirit."— (Zuck 1991, 23)

of the text? Are we to understand Paul as saying that without the "Spirit," the Bible and its teachings are beyond our understanding?

We can gain a measure of understanding as to what Paul meant, by observing how he uses the term "foolishness" elsewhere in the very same letter. At 1 Corinthians 3:19, it is used in the following way, "For the wisdom of this world is foolishness with God." This verse helps us to arrive at the use in two stages: (1) the verse states that human wisdom is foolishness with God, (2) and we know that the use of foolishness here does not mean that God cannot understand (or grasp) human wisdom. The use is that He sees human wisdom as 'foolish' and rejects it as such.

Therefore, the term "foolishness" of 1 Corinthians 3:19 is not in reference to not "understanding," but as to one's view of the text, its significance, or better yet, lack of significance, or lack of value. We certainly know that God can understand the wisdom of the world, but condemns it as being 'foolish.' The same holds true of 1 Corinthians 1:20, where the verbal form of foolishness is used, "Has not God made foolish the wisdom of the world?" Thus, we have the term "foolishness" being used before and after 1 Corinthians 2:14, (1:20; 3:19). In all three cases, we are dealing with the significance, the value being attributed to something.

Thus, it seems obvious that we should attribute the same meaning to our text in question, 1 Corinthians 2:14. In other words, the Apostle Paul, by his use of the term "foolishness," is not saying that the unbeliever is unable to understand, to grasp the Word of God. If this were the case, why would we ever share the Word of God, the gospel message with an unbeliever? Unbelievers can understand the Word of God; however, unbelievers see it as foolish, having no value or significance. The resultant meaning of chapters 1-3 of 1 Corinthians is that unbelieving world of mankind can understand the Word of God, but views it foolish (lacking value or significance); while God on the other hand understands the wisdom of the world of mankind, but views it foolish (lacking value or significance). Therefore, in both cases, the information is understood or grasped; however, it is rejected because to the party considering it, believes it lacks value or significance.

We pray for the guidance of the Holy Spirit, and our spirit, or mental disposition, needs to be attuned to God and His Spirit through study and application. Now, if our mental disposition is not in tune with the Spirit, we will not come away with the right answer. As Ephesians shows, we can grieve the Spirit.

Ephesians 4:30 English Standard Version (ESV)

[30] And do not **grieve the Holy Spirit** of God, by whom you were sealed for the day of redemption.

How do we grieve the Holy Spirit? We do that by acting contrary to its leading through deception, human weaknesses, imperfections, setting our figurative heart on something other than the leading.

Ephesians 1:18 English Standard Version (ESV)

[18] having the **eyes of your hearts** enlightened, that you may know what is the hope to which he has called you, what are the riches of his glorious inheritance in the saints,

"Eyes of your heart" is a Hebrew Scripture expression, meaning spiritual insight, to grasp the truth of God's Word. So we could pray for the guidance of God's Spirit, and at the same time, we can explain why there are so many different understandings (many wrong answers), some of which contradict each other, as being human imperfection that is diluting some of those interpreters, causing them to lose the Spirit's guidance.

A person sits down to study and prays earnestly for the guidance of Holy Spirit, that his mental disposition be in harmony with God's Word [or simply that his heart be in harmony with . . .], and sets out to study a chapter, an article, something biblical. In the process of that study, he allows himself to be moved, not by a mental disposition in harmony with the Spirit, but by human imperfection, by way of his wrong worldview, his biases, his preunderstanding.[10] A fundamental of grammatical-historical interpretation is that that we are to look for the simple meaning, the basic meaning, the obvious meaning. However, when this one comes to a text that does not say what he wants it to say, he rationalizes until he has the text in harmony with his preunderstanding. In other words, he reads his presuppositions into the text,[11] as opposed to discovering the meaning that was in the text. Even though his Christian conscience was

---

[10] Preunderstanding is all of the knowledge and understanding that we possess before we begin the study of the text.

[11] Presupposition is to believe that a particular thing is so before there is any proof of it

tweaked at the true meaning, he ignored it, as well as his mental disposition that could have been in harmony with the Spirit, to get the outcome he wanted.

In another example, it may be that the text does mean what he wants, but this is only because the translation he is using is full of theological bias, which is **violating** grammar and syntax, or maybe textual criticism rules and principles that arrives at the correct reading. Therefore, when this student takes a deeper look, he discovers that it could very well read another way, and likely should because of the context. He buries that evidence beneath his conscience, and never mentions it when this text comes up in a Bible discussion. In other words, he is grieving the Holy Spirit, and loses it on this particular occasion.

Human imperfection, human weakness, theological bias, preunderstanding, and many other things could dilute the Spirit, or even grieve the Spirit, so that while one may be praying for assistance, he is not getting it, or has lost it, because one, some, or all of these things he is doing has grieved the Spirit.

Again, it is not that an unbeliever cannot understand what the Bible means; otherwise, there would be no need to witness to him.

Rather, he does not have the spiritual awareness to see the significance of studying Scripture. An unbeliever can look at "the setting in which the Bible books were written and the circumstances involved in the writing," as well as "studying the words and sentences of Scripture in their normal, plain sense," to arrive the meaning of a text. However, without having any spiritual awareness about themselves, they would not see the significance of applying it in their lives. 1 Corinthians 2:14 says, "The natural person does not **accept** [Gr., dechomai] the things of the Spirit of God." Dechomai means, "to welcome, accept or receive." Thus, the unbeliever may very well understand the meaning of a text, but just does not *accept*, *receive* or *welcome* it as truth.

Acts 17:10-11 English Standard Version (ESV)

[10] The brothers immediately sent Paul and Silas away by night to Berea, and when they arrived they went into the Jewish synagogue. [11] Now these Jews [the Beroeans] were more noble than those in Thessalonica; they received [dechomai] the word with all eagerness, examining the Scriptures daily to see if these things were so.

Unlike the natural person, the Beroeans accepted, received, or welcomed the Word of God eagerly. Paul said the Thessalonians "received [*dechomai*] the word in much affliction, with the joy of the Holy Spirit." (1 Thess. 1:6) In the beginning of a person's introduction to the good news, he will take in knowledge of the Scriptures (1 Tim. 2:3-4), which if his heart is receptive, he will begin to apply them in his life, taking off the old person and putting on the new person. (Eph. 4:22-24) Seeing how the Scriptures have begun to alter his life, he will start to have a genuine faith over the things he has learned (Heb. 11:6), repenting of his sins. (Acts 17:30-31) He will turn around his life, and his sins will be blotted out. (Acts 3:19) At some point, he will go to God in prayer, telling the Father that he is dedicating his life to him, to carry out his will and purposes. (Matt. 16:24; 22:37) This regeneration is the Holy Spirit working in his life, giving him a new nature, placing him on the path to salvation.—2 Corinthians 5:17.

A new believer will become "acquainted with the sacred writings, which are able to make [him] wise for salvation through faith in Christ Jesus." (2 Tim. 3:15) As the Bible informs us, the Scriptures are holy, and are to be viewed as such. If we are to acquire an accurate or full knowledge, to have the correct mental grasp of the things that we carried out an exegetical analysis on, it must be done with a prayerful and humble heart. It is as Dr. Norman L. Geisler said, "the role of the Holy Spirit, at least in His special work on believers related to Scripture, is in illuminating our understanding of the significance (not the meaning) of the text. The meaning is clear apart from any special work of the Holy Spirit." What level of understanding that we are able to acquire is based on the degree to which we are **not** grieving the Holy Spirit with our worldview, our preunderstanding, our presuppositions, our theological biases. In addition, anyone living in sin will struggle to grasp God's Word as well.

No interpreter is infallible. The only infallibility or inerrancy belonged to the original manuscripts. Each Christian has the right to interpret God's Word, to discover what it means, but this does not guarantee that they will come away with the correct meaning. The Holy Spirit will guide us into and through the truth, by way of our working in behalf of our prayers to have the correct understanding. Our working in harmony with the Holy Spirit means that we buy out the time for a personal study program, not to mention the time to prepare properly and carefully for our Christian meetings. In these studies, do not expect that the Holy Spirit is going to miraculously give us some flash of understanding, but rather understanding will come to us as we set aside our personal biases, worldviews, human imperfections, presuppositions, preunderstanding, opening our mental disposition to the Spirit's leading as we study.

The Work of the Holy Spirit

The following is adopted and adapted from Douglas A. Foster of Abilene Christian University.

Christian Publishing House's understanding of the Holy Spirit is **not** that of the Charismatic groups (the ecstatic and irrational), but rather the calm and rational. The work of the Holy Spirit is inseparably and uniquely linked to the words and ideas of God's inspired and inerrant Word. We see the indwelling of the Holy Spirit as Christians taking the words and ideas of Scripture into our mind and drawing spiritual strength from them. The Spirit moves persons toward salvation, but the Spirit does that, in the same way, any person moves another—by persuasion with words and ideas:

Now we cannot separate the Spirit and the Word of God, and ascribe so much power to the one and so much to the other; for so did not the Apostles. Whatever the word does, the Spirit does, and whatever the Spirit does in the work of converting, the word does. We neither believe nor teach abstract Spirit nor abstract word, but word and Spirit, Spirit and word. But the Spirit is not promised to any persons outside of Christ. It is promised only to them who believe and obey him.[12]

The Holy Spirit works only through the word in the conversion of sinners. In other words, the Spirit acting through the Word of God can accomplish everything claimed to be effected by a personal indwelling of the Spirit.

longtime preacher Z. T. (Zachary Taylor) Sweeney, in His book *The Spirit and the Word: A Treatise on the Holy Spirit in the Light of a Rational Interpretation of the Word of God*, writes after examining every Scripture that might be used by advocates of a literal personal indwelling of the Holy Spirit,

---

[12] Alexander Campbell, The Christian System (6th ed.; Cincinnati: Standard, 1850), 64.

In the above cases, we have covered all the conceivable things a direct indwelling Spirit could do for one, and have also shown that all these things the Spirit does through the word of God. It is not claimed that a direct indwelling of the Spirit makes any new revelations, adds any new reasons or offers any new motives than are found in the word of God. Of what use, then, would a direct indwelling Spirit be? God makes nothing in vain. We are necessarily, therefore, led to the conclusion that, in dealing with his children today, God deals with them in the same psychological way that he deals with men in inducing them to become children. This conclusion is strengthened by the utter absence of any test by which we could know the Spirit dwells in us, if such were the case.[13]

Christian Publishing House is defined by our rejection of Holiness and Pentecostal understandings of the Holy Spirit. The Holy Spirit transforms a person,

---

[13] Z. T. Sweeney, The Spirit and the Word (Nashville: Gospel Advocate, n.d.), 121–26.

empowering him through the Word of God, to put on the "new person" required of true Christians: "So, as those who have been chosen of God, holy and beloved, put on a heart of compassion, kindness, humility, gentleness and patience."—Col. 3:12.

Ephesians 4:20-24 English Standard Version (ESV)

[20] But that is not the way you learned Christ!—[21] assuming that you have heard about him and were taught in him, as the truth is in Jesus, [22] to put off your old self, which belongs to your former manner of life and is corrupt through deceitful desires, [23] and to be renewed in the spirit of your minds, [24] and to put on the new self, created after the likeness of God in true righteousness and holiness.

Colossians 3:9-10 English Standard Version (ESV)

[9] Do not lie to one another, seeing that you have put off the old self with its practices [10] and have put on the new self, which is being renewed in knowledge after the image of its creator.

CHAPTER 3 How Are We to Understand the Indwelling of the Holy Spirit?

Edward D. Andrews

1 Corinthians 3:16 New American Standard Bible (NASB)

¹⁶ Do you not know that you are a temple of God and *that* the Spirit of God dwells in you?

Before delving into the phrase, "indwelling of the Holy Spirit, let us consider the words of New Testament scholars Simon J. Kistemaker and William Hendriksen, who write,

> The Spirit of God lives within you."
> The church is holy because God's Spirit dwells in the hearts and lives of the believers. In 6:19 Paul indicates that the Holy Spirit lives in the physical bodies of the believers. But now he tells the Corinthians that the presence of the Spirit is within them and they are the temple of God.

> The Corinthians should know that they have received the gift of God's Spirit. Paul had already called attention to the fact that they had not received

the spirit of the world but the Spirit of God (2:12). He teaches that Christians are controlled not by sinful human nature but by the Spirit of God, who is dwelling within them (Rom. 8:9).

The behavior—strife, jealousy, immorality, and permissiveness—of the Christians in Corinth was reprehensible. By their conduct the Corinthians were desecrating God's temple and, as Paul writes in another epistle, were grieving the Holy Spirit (Eph. 4:30; compare 1 Thess. 5:19).[14]

First, it must be said that I am almost amazed at how so many Bible scholars say nonsensical things, contradictory things when it comes to the Holy Spirit. Commentators use many verses to say that the Holy Spirit literally **(1) dwells in** the individual Christian believers, **(2)** having **control over** them, **(3) enabling them** to live a

---

[14] Simon J. Kistemaker and William Hendriksen, *Exposition of the First Epistle to the Corinthians*, vol. 18, New Testament Commentary (Grand Rapids: Baker Book House, 1953–2001), 117

righteous and faithful life,[15] with the believer **(4) still being able to sin**, even to the point of grieving the Holy Spirit (Eph. 4:30).

Let us walk through this again, and please take it slow, ponder whether it makes sense, is reasonable, logical, even Scriptural. The Holy Spirit literally dwells in individual believers, controlling them so they can live a righteous and faithful life, yet they can still freely sin, even to the point of grieving the Holy Spirit. Does this mean that the Holy Spirit is not powerful enough to prevent their sinful nature from affecting them? The commentators say the Holy Spirit now controls the Christian, not their sinful nature. If that were true, it must mean the Holy Spirit is ineffectual and less powerful than their sinful nature of the Christian, because the Christian can still reject the Holy Spirit and sin to the point of grieving the Holy Spirit. If the Holy Spirit is controlling the individual Christian, how is it possible that he still possesses free will?

Let us return to the phrase of "indwelling of the Holy Spirit." Just how often do we find "indwelling" in the Bible? I have looked at over

---

[15] Millard J. Erickson, *Introducing Christian Doctrine* (Grand Rapids: Baker Book House, 1992), 265–270

fifty English translations and found it once in the King James Version ad two in an earlier version of the New American Standard Version. One reference is to sin dwelling within us and the other reference is to the Holy Spirit dwelling within us. The 1995 Updated New American Standard Version removed such usage. We may be asking ourselves, since "indwelling" is almost nonexistent in the Scriptures, why the commentaries, Bible encyclopedias, Hebrew and Greek word dictionaries, Bible dictionaries, pastors and Christians using it to such an extent, especially in reference to the Holy Spirit. I say in reference to the Holy Spirit because some scholars refer to the indwelling of Christ and the Word of God.

Before addressing those questions, we must take a look at the Greek word behind 1 Corinthians 3:16 "the Spirit of God **dwells [οἰκέω]** in you." The transliteration of our Greek word is *oikeo*. It means "'to dwell' (from *oikos*, 'a house'), 'to inhabit as one's abode,' is derived from the Sanskrit, *vic*, 'a dwelling place' (the Eng. termination —'wick' is connected). It is used (a) of God as 'dwelling' in light, 1 Tim. 6:16; (b) of the 'indwelling' of the Spirit of God in the believer, Rom. 8:9, 11, or in a church, 1 Cor. 3:16; (c) of the 'indwelling' of sin, Rom. 7:20; (d) of the absence of any good thing in the flesh of the believer, Rom. 7:18; (e) of the 'dwelling' together of those who are married, 1 Cor. 7:12-13."[16]

Thus, for our text, means the Holy Spirit dwelling in true Christians. The TDNT tells us, "Jn.'s μένειν [menein] corresponds to Paul's οἰκεῖν [oikein], cf. Jn. 1:33: καταβαῖνον καὶ μένον ἐπ' αὐτόν [descending and remaining upon him]. The new possession of the Spirit is more than ecstatic."[17] What does TDNT mean? It means that John is using meno ("to remain," "to stay" or "to abide") in the same way that Paul is using oikeo ('to dwell').

When we are considering the Father or the Son alone, and even the Father and the Son together, we are able to have a straightforward conversation. However, when we get to the Holy Spirit we tend to get off into mysterious and mystical thinking. When we think of humans and the words *dwell* and *abide*, both have the sense of where we 'live or reside in a

---

[16] W. E. Vine, Merrill F. Unger, and William White Jr., *Vine's Complete Expository Dictionary of Old and New Testament Words* (Nashville, TN: T. Nelson, 1996), 180.

[17] Gerhard Kittel, Geoffrey W. Bromiley, and Gerhard Friedrich, eds., *Theological Dictionary of the New Testament* (Grand Rapids, MI: Eerdmans, 1964–)

place.' However, there is another sense of 'where we might stand on something,' 'our position on something.' Thus, in English dwell and abide can be used interchangeably, similarly, just as Paul and John use *meno* "abide" or "remain" and *oikeo* "dwell" similarly. Let us look at the apostle John's use of meno,

1 John 4:16

[16] So we have come to know and to believe the love that God has for us. God is love, and whoever **abides [meno]** in love abides in God, and God **abides [meno]** in him.

Here we notice that God is the embodiment of "love" and if we **abide in** or **remain in** that love, God then **abides in** or **remain in** us. We do not attach any mysterious or mystical sense to this verse, such as God literally being in us and us being in God. If we suggest that this verse, i.e., God being in us, means his taking control of our lives, does our being in God, also mean we control his life? We would think to suggest such a thing is unreasonable, illogical, nonsensical, and such. Commentator Max Anders in the *Holman New Testament Commentary* says, "This is the test of true Christianity in the letters of John. We must recognize the basic character of God, rooted in love. We must experience that love in our own relationship with God. Others must experience this God kind of love in their relationships with us." (Walls and Anders 1999, 211) Our love for God and man is the motivating factor in what we do and not do as Christians. John is saying that we need to remain in that love if we are to remain in God and God is to remain in us. We may be thinking, well, is it not true that God guides and direct us? Yes, however, this is because we have given our lives over to him.

1 John 2:14

14 I write to you, fathers,

because you know him who is from the beginning.

I write to you, young men,

because you are strong,

and the word of God **abides [*meno*]** in you,

and you have overcome the evil one.

Here we see that the Word of God abides or remains in us. Does this mean that the Word of God is literally within our body, controlling us? No, this means that our love for God and our love for his Word is a motivating factor in our walk with God. We are one with the Father as Jesus was and is one with the Father and he is one with us. Listen to the words of Paul in the book of Hebrews,

Hebrews 4:12

¹² For the word of God is living and active, sharper than any two-edged sword, piercing to the division of soul and of spirit, of joints and of marrow, and discerning the thoughts and intentions of the heart.

Is the Word of God literally living, and animate thing? No, it is an inanimate object. Is our Bible literally sharper than a sword? No, if we decide to stab someone with it, it would look quite silly. Is the Word of God literally able to pierce our joints and marrow? No, again, this would look silly. If we literally hold the Bible up to our head, is it able to discern our thinking, what we are intending to do? What did Paul mean? The Word of God does these things by our being able to evaluate ourselves by looking into the light of the Scriptures, which helps us to identify the intentions of our heart, i.e., inner person. When we meditatively read God's Word daily and ponder what the author meant, we are taking into our mind, God's thoughts and intentions. When we accept the Bible as the inspired, inerrant Word of God, take its counsel and apply its principles in our lives, it will have an impact on our conscience, the moral code that God gave Adam and Eve, our mental power or ability that enables us to reason between what is good and what is bad. (Rom 9:1) Then, the inner voice within us is not entirely ours, but is also God's Word, empowering us to avoid choosing the wrong path.

1 John 2:24

²⁴ Let what you heard from the beginning **abide [*meno*]** in you. If what you heard from the beginning **abides [*meno*]** in you, then you too will **abide [*meno*]** in the Son and in the Father.

Those who had followed Jesus **from the beginning** of his three and half ministry cleaved to what they had heard about the Father and the Son. Therefore, if the same truths are within our heart, inner person, our mental power or ability, we too can **abide** or **remain [*meno*]** in the Son and the Father. (John 17:3) It is as James said, if we draw close to God, through his Word the Bible, he will draw close to us. (Jam. 4:8) In other words, God becomes a part of us and we a part of him through the Word of God that is "living and active, sharper than any two-edged sword, piercing to the division of soul and of spirit, of joints and of marrow, and discerning the thoughts and intentions of the heart."

In John chapter 14, we see this two-way relationship more closely. Jesus said, "Believe me that I am in the Father and the Father is in me, or else believe on account of the works themselves." **(14:11)** He also said, "In that day you will know that I am in my Father, and you in me, and I in you." **(14:20)** We see that the Father and Son have a close relationship, a relationship that we are invited to join.

All through the above discussion of the Father and the Son, we likely had no problem following the line of thought. However, once we interject the Holy Spirit, it is as though our common sense is thrown out. Christians know that the Father and the Son reside in heaven. They also understand that when we speak of the Word of God, the Father and the Son dwelling in us, it is in reference to our being one with them, our unified relationship, by way of the Word of God. However, when we contemplate the Holy Spirit, it is as though our mental powers shut down, and we enter the realms of the mysterious and mysticism. However, we just understood John **14:11** and **14:20**, i.e., how Jesus is in the Father, the Father in Jesus, and their being in us. So, let us now consider the verses that lie between verse **11** and **20**.

Jesus Promises the Holy Spirit

John 14:15-17 English Standard Version (ESV)

¹⁵ "If you love me, you will keep my commandments. ¹⁶ And I will ask the Father, and he will give you another Helper, to be with you forever, ¹⁷ even the Spirit of truth, whom the world cannot receive, because it neither sees him nor knows him. You know him, for he **dwells [meno]** with you and will be in you.

First, do we not find it a bit disconcerting that all along when looking at John's writings as to the Son and the Father abiding **[meno]** in one another, in us, and us in them, the translation rendered **meno** as abiding, but now that the Holy Spirit is mentioned, they render **meno** as "**dwell**."

Do these verses call for us to; drive off the path of reason, into the realms of mysteriousness and mysticism talk? No, these verses are very similar to our 1 John 2:24 that we dealt with above, but will quote again, "Let what you heard from the beginning **abide [meno]** in you. If what you heard from the beginning **abides [meno]** in you, then you too will **abide** **[meno]** in the Son and in the Father." In 1 John 2:24, we are told that if the Word of God that we heard from the beginning of being a Christian, **abides** **[meno]** in us, we will **abide** **[meno]** in the Son and the Father. In John 14:15-17, if we keep Jesus' commands, the Holy Spirit will **dwell**, actually **abide** **[meno]** in us. In all of this, the common denominator has been the Word of God, because it is what we are to take into our mind and heart, which will affect change in our person, and enable us to abide in the Father and the Son, and they in us, as well as the Holy Spirit abiding in us.

The Holy Spirit, through the spirit inspired, inerrant Word of God is the motivating factor for our taking off the old person and putting on the new person. (Eph. 4:20-24; Col. 3:8-9) It is also the tool used by God so that we can "be transformed by the renewal of your mind, so that you may approve what is the good and well-pleasing and perfect will of God." (Rom 12:2; See 8:9) *The Theological Dictionary of the New Testament* compares this line of thinking with Paul's reference, at Romans 7:20, to the "sin that dwells within me."

The dwelling of sin in man denotes its dominion over him, its lasting connection with his flesh, and yet also a certain distinction from it. The sin which dwells in me (ἡ οἰκοῦσα ἐν ἐμοὶ ἁμαρτία) is no passing guest, but by its continuous presence becomes the master of the house (cf. Str.-B., III, 239).[18] Paul can speak in just the same way, however, of the lordship of the Spirit. The community knows (οὐκ οἴδατε, a reference to catechetical instruction, 1 C. 3:16) that the Spirit of God dwells in the new man (ἐν ὑμῖν οἰκεῖ, 1 C. 3:16; R. 8:9, 11). This "dwelling" is more than ecstatic rapture or impulsion by a superior power.[19]

How does the Holy Spirit control a Christian? Certainly, some mysterious or mystical feeling does not control him.

Paul told the Christians in Rome,

Romans 12:2 English Standard Version (ESV)

² Do not be conformed to this world, but be transformed by **the renewal of your mind**, that by testing you may discern what is

---

[18] Str.-B. H. L. Strack and P. Billerbeck, *Kommentar zum NT aus Talmud und Midrasch*, 1922 ff.

[19] Gerhard Kittel, Geoffrey W. Bromiley, and Gerhard Friedrich, eds., *Theological Dictionary of the New Testament* (Grand Rapids, MI: Eerdmans, 1964–), 135

the will of God, what is good and acceptable and perfect.

Just how do we **renew our mind**? This is done by taking in an accurate knowledge of Biblical truth, which enables us to meet God's current standards of righteousness. (Titus 1:1) This Bible knowledge, if applied, will enable us to move our mind in a different direction, by filling the void, after having removed our former sinful practices, with the principles of God's Word, principles that guide our actions, especially ones that guide moral behavior.

Psalm 119:105 Lexham English Bible (LEB)

[105] Your word *is* a lamp to my feet

and a light to my path.

The Biblical truths that lay in between Genesis 1:1 and Revelation 22:21 will transform our way of thinking, which will in return affect our mood and actions and our inner person. It will be as the apostle Paul said to the Ephesians. We need to "to put off your old self, which belongs to your former manner of life and is corrupt through deceitful desires, and to be renewed in the spirit of your minds, and to put on the new self, created after the likeness of God in true righteousness and holiness. . . ." (Ephesians 4:22-24) This force that contributes to our acting or behaving in a certain way, for our best interest is internal.

Paul told the Christians in Colossae,

Colossians 3:9-11 English Standard Version (ESV)

⁹ Do not lie to one another, seeing that you have put off the old self with its practices ¹⁰ and have put on the new self, which is **being renewed in knowledge** after the image of its creator. ¹¹ Here there is not Greek and Jew, circumcised and uncircumcised, barbarian, Scythian, slave, free; but Christ is all, and in all.

Science has certainly taken us a long way in our understanding of how the mind works, but it is only a grain of sand on the beach of sand in comparison to what we do not know. We have enough in these basics to understand some fundamental processes. When we open our eyes to the light of a new morning, it is altered into and electrical charge by the time it arrives at the gray matter of our brain's cerebral cortex. As the sound of the morning birds reaches our gray matter, it arrives as electrical impulses. The rest of our senses (smell, taste, and touch) arrive as electrical currents in the brain's cortex as well. The white matter of our brain lies within the cortex of gray matter, used as a tool to send electrical messages to other cells within other parts of the gray matter. Thus, when anyone of our five senses detects danger, at the speed of light, a message is sent to the motor section, to prepare us for the needed action of either fight or flight.

Here lies the key to altering our way of thinking. Every single thought, whether it is conscious or subconscious makes an electrical path through the white matter of our brain, with a record of the thought and event. This holds true with our actions as well. If it is a repeated way of thinking or acting, it has no need to form a new path; it only digs a deeper, engrained, established path. This would explain how a factory worker who has been on the job for some time, gives little thought as he performs his repetitive functions each day, it becomes unthinking, automatic, mechanical. These repeated actions become habitual. There is yet another facet to be considered; the habits, repeated thoughts and actions become simple and effortless to repeat. Any new thoughts and actions are more difficult to perform, as there needs to be new pathways opened up.

The human baby starts with a blank slate, with a minimal amount of stable paths built in to survive those first few crucial years. As the boy grows into childhood, there is a flood of pathways established, more than all of the internet connections worldwide. Our five senses are continuously adding to the maze. Ps. 139:14: "I will give thanks to you, for I am fearfully and wonderfully made. . . ." (NASB) So, it could never be overstated as to the importance of the foundational thinking and behavior that should be established in our children from infancy forward.

Paul told the Christians in Ephesus,

Ephesians 4:20-24 English Standard Version (ESV)

20 But that is not the way you learned Christ!— 21 assuming that you have heard about him and were taught in him, as the truth is in Jesus, 22 to put off your old self, which belongs to your former manner of life and is corrupt through deceitful desires, 23 and to be **renewed in the spirit of your minds**, 24 and to put on the new self, created after the likeness of God in true righteousness and holiness.

How are we to understand being **renewed in the spirit of our minds**? Christian living is carried out through the study and application of God's Word, in which, our spirit (mental disposition), is in harmony with God's Spirit.

Our day-to-day decisions are made with a biblical mind, a biblically guided conscience, and a heart that is motivated by love of God and neighbor. Because we have,

- Received the Word of God,
- treasured up the Word of God,
- have been attentive to the Word of God,
- inclining our heart to understanding the Word of God,
- calling out for insight into the Word of God,
- raising our voice for understanding of the Word of God,
- sought the Word of God like silver,
- have searched for the Word of God like gold,
- we have come to understand the fear of God, and have found the very knowledge of God, which now leads and directs us daily in our Christian walk.

Proverbs 23:7 New King James Version (NKJV)

⁷ For as he thinks in his heart, so is he. "Eat and drink!" he says to you, But his heart is not

with you. [Our thinking affects our emotions, which in turn affects our behavior.]

Irrational thinking produces irrational feelings, which will produce wrong moods, leading to wrong behavior. It may be difficult for each of us to wrap our mind around it, but we are very good at telling ourselves outright lies and half-truths, repeatedly throughout each day. In fact, some of us are so good at it that it has become our reality and leads to mental distress and bad behaviors.

When we couple our leaning toward wrongdoing with the fact that Satan the devil, who is "the god of this world," (2 Co 4:4) has worked to entice these leanings, the desires of the fallen flesh; we are even further removed from our relationship with our loving heavenly Father. During these 'last days, grievous times' has fallen on us as Satan is working all the more to prevent God's once perfect creation to achieve a righteous standing with God and entertaining the hope of eternal life.—2 Timothy 3:1-5.

When we enter the pathway of walking with our God, we will certainly come across resistance from three different areas (Our sinful nature, Satan and demons, and the world that caters to our flesh). **Our greatest obstacle** is

ourselves, because we have inherited imperfection from our first parents Adam and Eve. The Scriptures make it quite clear that we are **mentally bent toward bad**, not good. (Gen 6:5; 8:21, AT) In other words, our natural desire is toward wrong. Prior to sinning, Adam and Eve were perfect, and they had the natural desire of doing good, and to go against that was to go against the grain of their inner person. Scripture also tells us of our inner person, our heart.

Jeremiah 17:9 Lexham English Bible (LEB)

⁹ The **heart *is* deceitful** more than anything else,

and it *is* disastrous. Who can understand it?

Jeremiah's words should serve as a wakeup call, if we are to be pleasing in the eyes of our heavenly Father, we must focus on our inner person. Maybe we have been a Christian for many years; maybe we have a deep knowledge of Scripture, maybe we feel that we are spiritually strong, and nothing will stumble us. Nevertheless, our heart can be enticed by secret desires, where he fails to dismiss them; he eventually commits a serious sin.

Our conscious thinking (aware) and subconscious thinking (present in our mind without our being aware of it) originates in the mind. For good, or for bad, our mind follows certain rules of action, which if entertained one will move even further in that direction until they are eventually consumed for good or for bad. In our imperfect state, our bent thinking will lean toward wrong, especially with Satan using his world, with so many forms of entertainment that simply feeds the flesh.

James 1:14-15 Updated American Standard Version

[14] But each one is tempted when he is carried away and enticed by his own desire.[20] [15] Then the desire when it has conceived gives birth to sin, and sin when it is fully grown brings forth death.

1 John 2:16 Lexham English Bible (LEB)

[16] because everything *that is* in the world, the desire of the flesh and the desire of the eyes and the arrogance of material possessions—is not from the Father, but is from the world.

Matthew 5:28 Lexham English Bible (LEB)

---

[20] Or "own *lust*"

28 But I say to you that everyone who looks at a woman to lust for her has already committed adultery with her in his heart.

1 Peter 1:14 Lexham English Bible (LEB)

[14] As obedient children, do not be conformed to the former desires *you used to conform to*[21] in your ignorance

If we do not want to be affected by the world of humankind around us, which is alienated from God, we must again consider the words of the Apostle Paul's. He writes (Rom 12:2) "Do not be conformed to this world, but be transformed by the renewal of your mind that by testing you may discern what is the will of God, what is good and acceptable and perfect." Just how do we do that? This is done by taking in an accurate knowledge of Biblical truth, which enables us to meet God's current standards of righteousness. (Titus 1:1) This Bible knowledge, if applied, will enable us to move our mind in a different direction, by filling the void with the principles of God's Word, principles that guide our actions, especially ones that guide moral behavior.

Psalm 119:105 Lexham English Bible (LEB)

---

[21] This is an understood repetition of the earlier verb "be conformed to"

105 Your word *is* a lamp to my feet

and a light to my path.

The Biblical truths that lay in between Genesis 1:1 and Revelation 22:21 will transform our way of thinking, which will in return affect our mood and actions and our inner person. It will be as the apostle Paul set it out to the Ephesians. We need to "to put off your old self, which belongs to your former manner of life and is corrupt through deceitful desires, and to be renewed in the spirit of your minds, and to put on the new self, created after the likeness of God in true righteousness and holiness. . . ." (Ephesians 4:22-24) This force that contributes to our acting or behaving in a certain way, for our best interest is internal.

Bringing This Transformation About

The mind is the mental ability that we use in a conscious way to garner information and to consider ideas and come to conclusions. Therefore, if we perceive our realities based on the information, that surrounds us, generally speaking, most are inundated in a world that reeks of Satan's influence. This means that our perception, our attitude, thoughts, speech and conduct are in opposition to God and his Word. Most are in true ignorance to the changing power of God's Word. The apostle Paul helps us to appreciate the depths of those who reflect this world's disposition. He writes,

Ephesians 4:17-19 Lexham English Bible (LEB)

[17] This therefore I say and testify in the Lord, *that* you no longer walk as the Gentiles [unbelievers] walk: in the futility of their mind [emptiness, idleness, vanity, foolishness, purposelessness], [18] being darkened in understanding[mind being the center of human perception], alienated from the life of God[not Godless, but less God], because of the ignorance *that* is in them [due not to a lack of opportunity but deliberate rejection], because of the hardness of their heart [hardening as if by calluses, unfeeling], [19] who, becoming callous, gave themselves over to licentiousness, for the pursuit of all uncleanness in greediness.

Hebrews 4:12 Lexham English Bible (LEB)

[12] For the word of God *is* living and active and sharper than any double-edged sword, and piercing as far as the division of soul and spirit, both joints and marrow, and able to judge the reflections and thoughts of the heart.

By taking in this knowledge of God's Word, we will be altering our way of thinking, which will affect our emotions and behavior, as well as our lives now and for eternity. This Word will influence our minds, making corrections in the way we think. If we are to have the Holy Spirit controlling our lives, we must 'renew our mind' (Rom. 12:2) "which is being renewed in knowledge" (Col. 3:10) of God and his will and purposes. (Matt 7:21-23; See Pro 2:1-6) All of this boils down to each individual Christian digging into the Scriptures in a meditative way, so he can 'discover the knowledge of God, receiving wisdom; from God's mouth, as well as knowledge and understanding.' (Pro. 2:5-6) As he acquires the mind that is inundated with the Word of God, he must also,

James 1:22-25 English Standard Version (ESV)

22 But be doers of the word, and not hearers only, deceiving yourselves. **23** For if anyone is a hearer of the word and not a doer, he is like a man who looks intently at his natural face[22] in a mirror.

24 for he looks at himself and goes away, and immediately forgets what sort of man he was. **25** But he that looks into the perfect law, the law of liberty, and abides by it, being no

---

[22] Lit *the face of his birth*

hearer who forgets but a doer of a work, he
will be blessed in his doing.

CHAPTER 4 The Holy Spirit in the First Century and Today

Acts 4:31 Updated American Standard Version (UASV)

31 And when they had prayed, the place in which they were gathered together was shaken, and **they were all filled with the Holy Spirit** and **began to speak the word of God with boldness**.

Just three days before Jesus was executed, Jesus told his disciples, "And this gospel of the kingdom will be proclaimed in all the inhabited earth[23] as a testimony to all the nations, and then the end will come." (Matt. 24:14) Jesus would speak on this again just before he ascended to heaven, Jesus said to his disciples, "Go therefore and make disciples of all the nations … teaching them to observe all that I commanded you …" (Matt 28:19-20) Of course, being curious, they were asking him, "Lord, is it at this time you are restoring the kingdom to Israel?" He said to them, "It is not for you to know times or seasons that the Father has fixed by his own authority. But you

---

[23] Or *in the whole world*

75

will receive power when the Holy Spirit has come upon you; and you will be my witnesses in both Jerusalem and in all Judea and Samaria, and to the extremity of the earth."—Acts 1:6-8

It has been and will be mentioned several times in this publication, Christianity has lost its way in the great commission of proclaiming the good news of the kingdom, teaching biblical truths, and making disciples, even in the face of centuries of intensified missionary work this is true. It is the mission of Christian Publishing House and this author that the first-century lifesaving work of evangelism is restored, so that, all Christians may play a role in making disciples. Therefore, it is tools like this publication and others by this author and other authors, which will enable any willing Christian to share biblical truths effectively within their family, their community, their workplace or their school, to make disciples. Within this chapter, we will cover how the Holy Spirit can enable us to be bold when we are sharing biblical truths with others.[24]

---

[24] A recommend read THE HOLY SPIRIT AND THE CHRISTIAN How Are We to Understand the Work of and the Indwelling of the Holy Spirit? by Edward D. Andrews

The Need to Be Bold

One can only imagine the joy of making a disciple for Christ, who, in turn, goes out to make disciples himself. Congregation Evangelists, be it male or female should be very involved in evangelizing their communities and helping the church members play their role at the basic levels of evangelism. There is nothing to say that one church could not have many within, who have the calling of an evangelist, which would and should be cultivated. However, like in the first-century, we in the twenty-first-century have many challenges that get in our way. Generally speaking, few today are eager to hear from God's Word, mostly because the majority have preconceived ideas about it (just a man's book, full of errors and contradictions, and the like), many are of the same mindset as those who were living the days of Noah. "For as in those days before the flood they were eating and drinking, marrying and giving in marriage, until the day that Noah entered the ark." (Matt. 24:38-39, NASB) Then, the apostle Peter warned,

---

2 Peter 3:3-4 New American Standard Bible (NASB)

³ Know this first of all, that in the last days mockers will come with *their* mocking, following after their own lusts, ⁴ and saying, "Where is the promise of His coming? For *ever* since the fathers fell asleep, all continues just as it was from the beginning of creation."

On these verses, David Walls writes, "**In the last days** refers to all the days between the first advent of the Messiah and the second advent. Characteristic of that time frame, however long it will be, is the fact that people will make fun of the doctrine of the Second Coming. **Scoffing** toward Christians is to express derision or scorn about a Christian or Christianity, the Bible, or God. It describes the characteristic attitude of the day toward the Second Coming. False teachers argued that the promise of the Second Coming had been delayed so long that we may safely conclude that it would never happen. As far as they could see, the world was going on just as it always had–people lived and died, but nothing really changed." (Walls and Anders 1996, p. 141) Today, we have false teachers on both sides of the second coming fence: (1) ones that scoff at the idea of Jesus' second coming and

(2) those that act as though they are prophets of God, knowing the very day and hour.[25] However, we also have those that from liberal and moderate "Christianity" that ridicule, mock and oppose conservative Christianity. All of this, and we have not even gotten to those outside of Christianity, who also ridicule, mock and oppose the Almighty God and his Word, the Bible.

As true Christians, we may face ridicule, mocking and opposition from the governmental officials, the news and entertainment media, other religions, and the agnostics and atheists. However, even more close to home, it may come from those that our children go to school with, their teachers or it may come from those we work with, even from close family members. All of these people need evangelized to if we are to carry out the Great Commission of proclaiming and teaching God's Word, to make disciples for Christ. We need to evangelize those in false forms of

---

[25] A recommended read WHAT DOES THE BIBLE REALLY SAY ABOUT THE SECOND COMING OF CHRIST? by Edward D. Andrews

http://www.christianpublishers.org/apps/webstore/products/show/5383701

"Christianity," the unbelievers and those in either of these categories, who are closer to us.

However, we face yet more challenges that are in our way. One such challenge is our human imperfection, i.e., our human weaknesses, such as shyness and fear of being ridiculed, mocked and opposed. Lastly, our greatest obstacle is our church leaders, who are failing to train us to be effective evangelizers in our communities. James, Jesus' half-brother wrote, "One of you says to them [the poor], 'Go in peace, be warmed and filled,'" without giving them the things needed for the body, what good is that? So also faith by itself, if it does not have works, is dead." (Jam. 2:16-17, ESV) This principle can be carried over to pastors, elders, priests, ministers, who say to their congregation, "**You** need to share the gospel in **your** community, so that **you** may help build up the church for Christ." All of this pointing the finger at them by using the second person pronoun, "**you**" repeatedly, and these leaders have not even given them the tools to be effective evangelists within their community. What good is that? Therefore, their supposed faith that the evangelism work will be done, but having no works of training such ones, means they have no genuine faith at all, it is dead. If we are to persist in sharing the Word of

God, this will require that we have the tools to help us (i.e., this book and others like it), as well as boldness. In this chapter, we will focus on boldness.

Ephesians 6:19-20 Updated American Standard Version (UASV)

[19] and for me, that a word may be given to me at the opening of my mouth **boldly**, to make known the mystery of the gospel, [20] for which I am an ambassador in chains, that I may proclaim it **boldly**, as I ought to speak.

The Greek word, *parresia*, "boldness" in verse 19 has the sense of in boldness "in an evident or publicly known manner—'publicly, in an evident manner, well known.'"[26] The Greek word, *parresiazomai*, "boldly" in verse 19, is a "(derivative of *parresia* 'boldness,' 25.158) to speak openly about something and with complete confidence—'to speak boldly, to speak openly.'"[27] However, this boldness, confidence, courage, fearlessness does not give us a license to be blunt or rude to the ones we speak to, even if their demeanor is such. The

---

[26] Johannes P. Louw and Eugene Albert Nida, *Greek-English Lexicon of the New Testament: Based on Semantic Domains* (New York: United Bible Societies, 1996), 337.

[27] IBID., 398.

apostle said to the Christians in Rome, "Never pay back evil for evil to anyone." (Rom. 12:17; See Col. 4:6, NASB) He went on to say, "If possible, so far as it depends on you, be at peace with all men." (Rom. 12:18, NASB) When we go about our evangelism work, sharing God's Word with others, we need to be bold in this hostile world, but it needs to be balanced with tact as well, because our objective is not to offend the one we to whom we are witnessing.

To be sure, this sort of boldness calls for personal qualities that involve much effort that needs to be developed over time. We do not just wake up one morning and decide that we are going to be bold from here forward. In addition, we do not just read a couple Bible verses about being bold, and then, we are all of a sudden able to be bold in our witnessing to others. "But after we [Paul and his companions] had already suffered and been mistreated in Philippi, as you know, **we had the boldness in our God** to speak to you the gospel of God amid much conflict." (1 Thess. 2:2) We today can acquire a similar boldness if we are hesitant, shy or nervous at the idea of speaking to others about the Word of God.

Paul and his traveling companions had boldness, which you can note he said in the above, "we had the boldness in our God." In other words, God removed Paul's fears and gave him boldness. The rulers, elders, and scribes gathered in Jerusalem and commanded Peter and John to no longer witness about Jesus. These Jewish religious leaders had the power of life and death over them. Of course, they could only take their life, not their opportunity at eternal life. However, Peter and John answered them, "Whether it is right in the sight of God to listen to you rather than to God, you must judge, for we cannot but speak of what we have seen and heard." God was well aware of these threats, but he granted his servants to speak his word *"with all boldness."* Ac 4:5, 19-20, 29, ESV) The Father had provided them with Holy Spirit. What about us; Should we expect that the Holy Spirit under this direct and supernatural control will guide, lead, and direct us in the same bold way.

What Was the Reason for the Direct and Supernatural Work of the Holy Spirit in the First Century?

A significant change was in the offing. The Jews had followed the lead of their religious leaders in the last act of rebellion, resulting in their rejection as his people. The Mosaic Law was being replaced with the law of Christ. This does not mean that no Jew could be received into the newly founded Christian congregation. To the contrary, the next three and half years would be only the Jewish people, which would make up this new way to God. As was the case with Moses, there was to be a sign, miraculous events, which included the speaking in tongues, this as evidence to those, whose heart was receptive to the truth that the Son of God had come, had given his life for them, and ascended back to heaven. Exodus 19:16-19

However, there was much labor to be done. Beginning in 36 C.E., with the conversion of Cornelius, an uncircumcised Gentile, the gospel got underway in its spread to non-Jewish people of every nation. (Acts, chap. 10) In truth, so swiftly did it spread that by about 60 C.E., the apostle Paul could say that the gospel had been "proclaimed in all creation that is under heaven." (Col. 1:23) Consequently, by the time of the last apostles death (John c. 100 C.E.), Jesus' faithful followers had made disciples all the way through the Roman Empire—in Asia, Europe, and Africa! By 125 C.E., there were over one million Christians.

If we objectively look at the history of first-century Christianity, the three and a half year ministry of Jesus, founding the Christian congregation, the apostles spreading the good news throughout the whole of the Roman Empire, and the Holy Spirit miraculously guiding, leading and showing the apostles the "things to come," reminding them of all that Jesus had said. The apostles and a select few of others, like Paul, Barnabas, Silas, Apollos, Timothy, Titus, Philip, were under direct and supernatural control as they established Christianity in the first century. While there may have been a few individuals, attempting to cause division in the first century, by 100 C.E. there was but one Christianity, the one Jesus founded and the apostle grew. The twenty-seven books of the New Testament were to be added to the Old Testament by 200 C.E. The particular work of the Holy Spirit that Jesus spoke of had run its course by the death of the apostle John in 100 C.E., as he was the last apostle. After John, no man has been miraculously guided or directed, in the same manner and way, because that same specific work of the Holy Spirit was no longer needed. The work of the Holy Spirit from the second century forward has been within the inspired, inerrant Word of God. There was no need for the Holy Spirit to operate the same as in the first century because the work of setting up Christianity and completing the Word of God was completed.

The work of the Holy Spirit now takes place through the Spirit-inspired Word of God.

What Were the Gifts of the Holy Spirit in the First Century

What miraculous, supernatural gifts were the apostles and a select few workers to receive, to establish first century Christianity? They would receive a helper, comforter, an instructor, a guide, a supporter, i.e., the Holy Spirit. What did Jesus say about the Holy Spirit, being specifically applied to the apostles and a select few other fellow workers, to accomplish their work of establishing Christianity and completing the Bible? He had much to say on this, as we will discover from the texts below. Italics and underlines are mine.

John 14:15-17 Updated American Standard Version (UASV)

¹⁵ "If you love me, you will keep my commandments. ¹⁶ And I will ask the Father, and he will give you another Helper, that he may be with you forever; ¹⁷ the Spirit of truth, *whom the world cannot receive*, because it does not see him or know him, but you know him because *he dwells with <u>you</u>* and *will be in <u>you</u>*.

John 14:26 Updated American Standard Version (UASV)

²⁶ But the Helper, the Holy Spirit, whom the Father will send in my name, *that one will teach you* all *things* and *bring to your remembrance* all that I have said to you.

John 15:26 Updated American Standard Version (UASV)

²⁶ "But when the Helper comes, whom I will send to you from the Father, the Spirit of truth, who proceeds from the Father, *that one will bear witness about me*.

John 16:5-8 Updated American Standard Version (UASV)

⁵ But now I am going to him who sent me, and none of you asks me, 'Where are you going?' ⁶ But because I have said these things to you, sorrow has filled your heart. ⁷ Nevertheless, I tell you the truth: it is to your advantage that I go away; for if I do not go away, the Helper will not come to you; but if I go, I will send him to you. ⁸ And when that one arrives, *he will convict the world concerning sin* and *righteousness* and *judgment*;

John 16:12-15 Updated American Standard Version (UASV)

¹² "I still have many things to say to you, but you cannot bear them now. ¹³ But when that one, the Spirit of truth, comes, *he will*

guide you into all the truth; for he will not speak from himself, but whatever he hears, he will speak; and *he will declare to you the things that are to come.* **14** That one will glorify me, for *he will take what is mine and declare it to you.* **15** All the things that the Father has are mine; therefore I said that he takes what is mine and will declare it to you.

In the above texts, we have a number of things that the Holy Spirit was to do for the apostles and a select few other fellow workers. While the apostle were not ignorant or illiterate as some commentators suppose, they did not possess training in the Rabbinic study of Scripture, such as the apostle Paul had under Gamaliel. Luke tells us of an account of Peter and John before the Jewish religious leaders, where he writes,

Acts 4:13 Updated American Standard Version (UASV)

13 Now when they saw the boldness of Peter and John, and perceived that they were uneducated and untrained men, **they were astonished**, and they recognized that they had been with Jesus.

All of a sudden, Peter and John, literate fishermen were keeping pace with the Jewish religious leaders, who had training in the

Rabbinic study of Scripture. This is the Holy Spirit teaching them, guiding them, instructing them, bringing back to their remembrance all that Jesus had said. Therefore, the apostles and a select few fellow workers needed the Holy Spirit if they were to establish Christianity on the grand scale that it was by the end of the first century and complete the New Testament. There was no way that the apostles alone could have educated themselves to the level of Paul, in such a short period, it was the Holy Spirit, who taught and instructed them miraculously. The Holy Spirit guided them as well. One way was in their writings, as no New Testament author contradicted another; they were all one because there was really one author, God. This is actually true of all forty plus authors of the entire Bible. From the second century forward, this has never repeated. In fact, today we have 41,000 different denominations, all teaching different things on the same doctrines.

Convicting the World Concerning Sin

Nisan 14, 33 C.E., the night of the Passover feast with Jesus, he told the apostles, "When he [the Holy Spirit] comes, he will convict the world concerning sin and righteousness and judgment." (John 16:8, ESV) How did the Holy Spirit do this on Pentecost? The first stage was to baptize the apostle in Holy Spirit, which means that they would have been miraculously endowed with guidance, instruction, teachings, and a remembrance of what Jesus had said. Again, looking at Jesus' words just before his ascension, he said, "for John baptized with water, but you will be baptized with the Holy Spirit not many days from now." (Acts 1:5, ESV) The second stage was the work that these ones would carry out in the first century, namely, putting the world on notice (convicting them concerning their sin and righteousness), which was very similar to what the Mosaic Law had done with the Israelites. Remember the words of the apostle Paul,

Romans 5:20-21 New American Standard Bible (NASB)

20 The [Mosaic] Law came in so that the transgression would **increase**; but where sin increased, grace abounded all the more, 21 so that, as sin reigned in death, even so grace would reign through righteousness to eternal life through Jesus Christ our Lord.

How did the Mosaic Law make sin "increase"? From Adam's rebellion to the Mosaic Law, man was well aware of right and wrong because even in imperfection he had a sense of right and wrong. God had given Adam and Eve a conscience, an internal mechanism, to evidence the difference between right and wrong. In their perfection, they were able to sin still because even if a perfect person entertains bad thoughts, it will lead to sin and death. (Jam 1:14-15) Nevertheless, humankind in imperfection has a measure of that conscience that was given to Adam and Eve, meaning they have always had a sense of good and bad. However, the Mosaic Law laid our more explicitly what sin was and the different aspects of it. Therefore, the Mosaic Law caused sin to increase. On this Paul wrote,

Romans 7:7-8 New American Standard Bible (NASB)

⁷ What shall we say then? Is the Law sin? May it never be! On the contrary, I would not have come to know sin except through the Law; for I would not have known about coveting if the Law had not said, "You shall not covet." ⁸ But sin, taking opportunity through the commandment, produced in me coveting of every kind; for apart from the Law sin *is* dead.

Like the apostle Paul, neither Jewish persons nor us today, would know the full range of sin without the Mosaic Law. Paul gave us the example of coveting. The law exposed the coveting spirit that Paul would never have truly recognized in its fullest sense. This is how Paul could say, "apart from the Law sin *is* dead," specifically, it would not be as recognizable, as exposed, as highlighted. The Law made people more aware of the extent of their sinful nature. We should offer a word of caution, though, the Mosaic Law did not move them toward sin, or make sin more appealing, but rather it exposed sin for what it was. Sin is missing the mark of perfection. Sin is being out of harmony with the Creator, his personality, standards, and ways, which he inculcated in his creation. The Law made it possible to convict more people concerning sin. Now, the apostles, baptized in Holy Spirit were going to take this a step further with the law of Christ. Again, Jesus said to his apostles, "When he [the Holy Spirit] comes, he will convict the world [by way of the apostle workers] concerning sin and righteousness and judgment." (John 16:8, ESV)

What do we mean by 'convicting the world concerning sin'? This is not a reference to sin in general, as though, the Holy Spirit would personally come upon a person who just watched a movie they should not have, or they just told a lie, or they committed any sin. When we feel this inner guilt, a groaning of our inner person, because we know we have just done wrong, this is not the Holy Spirit convicting us of that sin. It is the Holy Spirit working through the Word of God, which convicts us of sin. Sin will cause us to feel guilt, anxiety, insecurity, shame. We get a clearer understanding of this when we consider Paul's words that "the work of the law is written on their hearts, while their conscience also bears witness, and their conflicting thoughts accuse or even excuse them." (Rom 2:15, ESV) In other words, when we fall short of God's standards as they are laid out in Scripture or our God given conscience, we will feel an internal groaning within us, which is our conscience convicting us of wrongdoing.

We are born with the weaker version of the conscience that God had given Adam and Eve. It will prevent most humans from committing the obvious right and wrongs, even if they never read the Word of God their entire life. However, considering that almost all of the teachers and professors in the United States and Especially Europe and Canada, are of a liberal progressive mindset, which is contrary to God's standards, the conscience is greatly weakened by Satan's world. If our conscience is ignored, it will become callused and unfeeling, no longer warning us of our wrongdoing, because it no longer wrongdoing in our heart and mind. On the other hand, if Scripture trains our conscience, it will not allow us to commit the wrongdoing in the first place. Returning to the being made bold by the Holy Spirit, we too can receive the Spirit in our evangelism work, but not in the same way and the same sense as the apostles and their fellow workers.

The Work of the Holy Spirit in the First Century

There was a different level of relationship between fist century Christianity and Christianity over the next 2,000 years. It must be remembered that Christ needed (1) **to train** those that would, (2) **establish Christianity**, and (3) **grow Christianity** to the point that it was **extensive** and **united**. This was needed to withstand the apostasy and false teachers that were to come over the next 2,000 years, who would split Christianity into so many factions, finding the truth and the way of the first century today is nigh impossible. All that Jesus and his apostles were to accomplish took place in a mere one hundred years while also publishing the twenty-seven books of the New Testament that later Christians would bring together as one book. There was a definite need for the Holy Spirit in first century

Christianity. Let us look at the gifts of prophesy and speaking in tongues.

As for Tongues, They Will Cease

1 Corinthians 13:8-10 English Standard Version (ESV)

⁸ Love never ends. As for prophecies, they will pass away; as for tongues, they will cease; as for knowledge, it will pass away. ⁹ For we know in part and we prophesy in part, ¹⁰ but when the perfect comes, the partial will pass away.

Some may argue that the evidence does not give one any idea of when the gift of tongues was to end. However, they would be mistaken in this case. There are three lines of evidence that present the fact that the gift of tongues would die out shortly after the death of the last apostle, which was the apostle John, who died about 98-100 C.E. **First**, the gift of tongues was always passed on to the person, only by an apostle: either by laying his hands on this one, or at least being present. (Acts 2:4, 14, 17; 10:44-46; 19:6; see also Acts 8:14-18.) **Second**, 1 Corinthians 13:8 informed the Corinthian reader specifically that this gift would "cease." In short, the Greek word for cease [*pausontai*], means to 'peter out,' or 'to die out,' not to be brought to a halt. We will deal with *pausontai* more extensively in a moment. **Third**, both one and two are exactly what happened when we look at the history of this gift of tongues. M'Clintock and Strong's *Cyclopaedia* (Vol. VI, p. 320) says that it is "an uncontested statement that during the first hundred years after the death of the apostles we hear little or nothing of the working of miracles by the early Christians." Therefore, following their passing off the scene and after those who in that way had obtained the gift of tongues breathed their last breath; the gift of tongues should have died out with these ones. (Elwell, 2001, 1207-8) This analysis concurs with the intention of those gifts as acknowledged at Hebrews 2:2-4. In other words, The gifts of the Spirit in the first century, which includes speaking in tongues, was evidence that God had abandoned the 1,600 years of the nation of Israel being the way to God to the Christian congregation.

Daniel B. Wallace in his *Greek Grammar Beyond the Basics* helps us to better comprehend how we are to understand *pausontai* of 1 Corinthians 13:8:

> If the voice of the verb here is significant, then Paul is saying either that tongues will cut themselves off (direct middle) or, more likely, cease of

their own accord, i.e., 'die out' without an intervening agent (indirect middle). It may be significant with reference to prophecy and knowledge, Paul used a different verb ([*katargeo*]) and out it in the passive voice. In vv 9-10, the argument continues: 'for we *know* in part and we *prophecy* in part; but when the perfect comes, the partial shall be done away with [*katargethesontai*].' Here again, Paul uses the same passive verb he had used with prophecy and knowledge and he speaks of the verbal counterpart to the nominal 'prophecy' and 'knowledge.' Yet he does not speak about *tongues* being done away 'when the perfect comes.' The implication *may* be that tongues were to have 'died out' on their own *before* the perfect comes. (Wallace 1996, 422)

These abilities were only established by the presence or lying on of hands by the apostles. This coincides with 1 Corinthians 13:8 and the history of these phenomena. Our Greek word for "cease" means that the gift of tongues was to 'die out' over time as the last of those who had received this gift passed off the scene of this earth. This is established by the historical fact that the second century saw just that being evidenced. Today, the Christian is moved by Spirit to speak with his heart and mind, defending and establishing the gospel, and destroying false doctrines, snatching some back from the fire. It is these things, which will give credence to the words of the modern-day Christian congregation: "God is really among you."–1 Corinthians 14:24-25.

The special, supernatural gifts, such as speaking in tongues gave impetus to the evangelism work that needed to be done in the first century, into many different lands throughout the Roman Empire. (Matt 28:19-20; Ac 1:8; 2:1-11) In the first century, the ones who spoke in tongues did so in languages that others could understand. (Ac 2:4, 8) If we look at those who claim to do so today, it is some ecstatic explosion of incomprehensible sounds, which only draws attention to them.

1 Corinthians 12:7-11 English Standard Version (ESV)

⁷ To each is given the manifestation of the Spirit for the common good. ⁸ For to one is given through the Spirit the utterance of wisdom, and to another the utterance of knowledge according to the same Spirit, ⁹ to another faith by the same Spirit, to another gifts

of healing by the one Spirit, ¹⁰ to another the working of miracles, to another prophecy, to another the ability to distinguish between spirits, to another various kinds of tongues, to another the interpretation of tongues. ¹¹ All these are empowered by one and the same Spirit, who apportions to each one individually as he wills.

What we see here mentioned by Paul, apparently does not take place today in any Christian congregation. He is indicating various direct and supernatural manifestations of the Spirit, which was a direct gift from the Holy Spirit. There was a reason for these miraculous gifts, which Paul mentions in his letter to the Ephesians,

Ephesians 4:11-13 Updated American Standard Version (UASV)

¹¹ And he gave some as apostles, and some as prophets, and some as evangelists, and some as shepherds and teachers, ¹² for the equipping of the holy ones or the work of ministry, to the building up of the body of Christ; ¹³ until we all attain to the unity of the faith, and of the knowledge of the Son of God, to a mature man, to the measure of the stature which belongs to the fullness of Christ.

If we look at the above mention history of the Christian congregation of the first century and what was accomplished, it perfectly fits Paul's reasons here. The reason for the direct gifts of the Holy Spirit was (1) **to train** those that would, (2) **establish Christianity**, and (3) **grow Christianity** to the point that it was **extensive** and **united**. This gift of the Spirit accompanied the baptism of the Spirit on the day of Pentecost. As has been mentioned, the 120 disciples in that upper room, grew to become a united, one denomination of Christianity, which numbered over one million all throughout the Roman Empire, after a mere century. Therefore, when Peter promised the gift of the Holy Spirit on the day of Pentecost, it **was not** to be universally given across the whole of Christianity until the return of Jesus Christ, applying to all who obeyed the Word of God. Rather, it was limited to those of the first century. Even so, it was the apostles and a select few fellow workers, who manifested the Holy Spirit in a supernatural way, by being miraculously taught, instructed, guided, and bringing to their remembrance exactly what Jesus taught for three and a half years, and what Jesus meant by the words that he used. Yes, there were a number, in the first century, who were used as apostles [those caring for many congregations], and some as prophets [those proclaiming God's Word], and some as evangelists [a proclaimer of the gospel or good news],[28] and some as shepherds [elders or overseers in the congregation] and teachers [those who teach within the congregation].

Philip the Evangelist

Philip preached the Word of God to the Samaritans in the city of Samaria after the great persecution arose following the death of Stephen.

Acts 8:12-17 English Standard Version (ESV)

[12] But when they believed Philip as he preached good news about the kingdom of

---

[28] Basic Evangelism is planting seeds of truth and watering any seeds that have been planted. [In the basic sense of this word (*euaggelistes*), this would involve all Christians.] In some cases, it may be that one Christian planted the seeds, which were initially rejected, so he was left in a good way because the planter did not try to force the truth down his throat. However, sometime later he faces something in life that moves him to reconsider those seeds, and some other Christian waters what had already been planted. This evangelism can be carried out in all of the methods that are available: informal, house-to-house, street, and the like. What amount of time is invested in the evangelism work is up to each Christian to decide for themselves.

God and the name of Jesus Christ, they were baptized, both men and women. ¹³ Even Simon himself believed, and after being baptized he continued with Philip. And seeing signs and great miracles performed, he was amazed.

¹⁴ Now when the apostles at Jerusalem heard that Samaria had received the word of God, they sent to them Peter and John, ¹⁵ who came down and prayed for them that they might receive the Holy Spirit, ¹⁶ for he had not yet fallen on any of them, but they had only been baptized in the name of the Lord Jesus. ¹⁷ Then they laid their hands on them and they received the Holy Spirit.

What do we notice here? We have Philip, a very important and prominent evangelist, who took the good news to Samaria. He preached and baptized the Samaritans. Philip was endowed with Holy Spirit with six other men, who were selected for a special service. "These [seven men] set before the apostles, and they prayed and **laid their hands on them**." (Ac 6:6) We see that Philip was able to perform signs and great miracles. If the gift of the Holy Spirit was to be for all who accepted Jesus and was baptized, why did the Samaritans not receive the Spirit? Philip was not an apostle, meaning he could not confer the gift of the Spirit by laying hands on them, even though he had had hands laid on him, and he could perform signs and great miracles. Therefore, Peter and John were dispatched to Samaria, to lay hands on the Samaritans, so that "they might receive the Holy Spirit." It should be noted that the gifts of the Holy Spirit were **always** conveyed to others by the apostles of Jesus Christ (1) laying on of hands (2) or in their presence.

The Holy Spirit Falls on the Gentile

Cornelius was a Gentile an army officer (centurion, KJV), who commanded 100 soldiers. He was "a devout man" who "feared God with all his household, gave alms generously to the people, and prayed continually to God," "an upright and God-fearing man, who is well spoken of by the whole Jewish nation." About the ninth hour of the day, he saw clearly in a vision an angel of God come in and say to him, "Cornelius." And he stared at him in terror and said, "What is it, Lord?" And he said to him, "Your prayers and your alms have ascended as a memorial before God." The angel also told Cornelius, "send men to Joppa and bring one Simon who is called Peter." (Acts 10:1-22) Again, the gifts of the Holy Spirit were always conveyed to others by the apostles of Jesus Christ (1) laying on of hands (2) or in their presence.

Acts 10:44-48 English Standard Version (ESV)

⁴⁴ While Peter was still saying these things, the Holy Spirit fell on all who heard the word. ⁴⁵ And the believers from among the circumcised who had come with Peter were amazed, because the gift of the Holy Spirit was poured out even on the Gentiles. ⁴⁶ For they were hearing them speaking in tongues and extolling God. Then Peter declared, ⁴⁷ "Can anyone withhold water for baptizing these people, who have received the Holy Spirit just as we have?" ⁴⁸ And he commanded them to be baptized in the name of Jesus Christ. Then they asked him to remain for some days.

Disciples at Ephesus

In Acts chapter 19, we find Paul meeting up with certain disciples that had been baptized by the John the Baptist. Paul explained that John was not aware of the full Gospel before his death. Below you will notice that these disciples of John had not even heard of the Holy Spirit, even though John pointed his disciples toward Jesus. Yet again, the gifts of the Holy Spirit were always conveyed to others by the apostles of Jesus Christ (1) laying on of hands (2) or in their presence.

Acts 19:1-7 English Standard Version (ESV)

¹ And it happened that while Apollos was at Corinth, Paul passed through the inland country and came to Ephesus. There he found some disciples. ² And he said to them, "Did you receive the Holy Spirit when you believed?" And they said, "No, we have not even heard that there is a Holy Spirit." ³ And he said, "Into what then were you baptized?" They said, "Into John's baptism." ⁴ And Paul said, "John baptized with the baptism of repentance, telling the people to believe in the one who was to come after him, that is, Jesus." ⁵ On hearing this, they were baptized in the name of the Lord Jesus. ⁶ And when Paul had laid his hands on them, the Holy Spirit came on them, and they began speaking in tongues and prophesying. ⁷ There were about twelve men in all.

Young Timothy

Here is yet another experience where someone has received the Holy Spirit by an apostle laying hands on him or her. Once more, the gifts of the Holy Spirit were always conveyed to others by the apostles of Jesus

Christ (1) laying on of hands (2) or in their presence.

2 Timothy 1:4-7 English Standard Version (ESV)

[4] As I remember your tears, I long to see you, that I may be filled with joy. [5] I am reminded of your sincere faith, a faith that dwelt first in your grandmother Lois and your mother Eunice and now, I am sure, dwells in you as well. [6] For this reason I remind you to fan into flame the gift of God, which is in you through the laying on of my hands, [7] for God gave us a spirit not of fear but of power and love and self-control.

Christian In Rome

That the gifts of the Holy Spirit were always conveyed to others by the apostles of Jesus Christ (1) laying on of hands (2) or in their presence was clear. Listen to the praise of Paul to these ones in Rome. He writes, "To all those in Rome who are loved by God and called to be holy ones: 'Grace to you and peace from God our Father and the Lord Jesus Christ. First, I thank my God through Jesus Christ for all of you, because your faith is proclaimed in all the world. For God is my witness, whom I serve with my spirit in the gospel of his

Son, that without ceasing I mention you always in my prayers, asking that somehow by God's will I may now at last succeed in coming to you.'" Paul goes on to tell these Christians.

Romans 1:11 New American Standard Bible (NASB)

¹¹ For I long to see you so that I may impart some spiritual gift to you, that you may be established;

Notice that Paul could encourage and counsel them from a distance in the longest letter he had penned. However, it was necessary that he be present to convey gifts of the Spirit by his presence or the laying on of hands.

What have we learned thus far? First, the gift of the Spirit was a miraculous, supernatural gift for helping the first century believers to be bold, to perform signs and miracles, to speak in foreign languages, to be Jesus' "witnesses in Jerusalem and in all Judea and Samaria, and to the end of the earth." (Ac 1:8) We also notice that the gifts of the Holy Spirit were **always** conveyed to others by the apostles of Jesus Christ (1) laying on of hands (2) or in their presence. Moreover, once the last apostle died, John, in 100 C.E., there was no longer one available to convey the gifts of the Spirit.

Therefore, the Greek word at 1 Corinthians 13:8 for "cease" [pausontai], became a reality in that the gifts that had been given 'petered out,' or 'died out,' namely, they were not brought to a halt, as some were, like prophecy. In other words, they died out as the last ones who were given them died at the beginning of the second century. Second, we can see from the letters of the New Testament authors that in the first century, many of the congregations were filled with members that had the supernatural power of the Spirit. Moreover, when we interpret those letters, this must be a part of the historical setting. Below are a few examples from these letters,

Romans 8:9, 23 English Standard Version (ESV)

⁹ You, however, are not in the flesh but **in the Spirit, if in fact the Spirit of God dwells in you**. Anyone who does not have the Spirit of Christ does not belong to him. ²³ And not only the creation, but **we** ourselves, who have **the firstfruits of the Spirit**, groan inwardly as we wait eagerly for adoption as sons, the redemption of our bodies.

Romans 15:30 English Standard Version (ESV)

³⁰ I appeal to you, brothers, by our Lord Jesus Christ and **by the love of the Spirit**, to strive together with me in your prayers to God on my behalf,

2 Corinthians 5:5 English Standard Version (ESV)

⁵ He who has prepared us for this very thing is God, who **has given us the Spirit as a guarantee**.

Ephesians 1:13-14 English Standard Version (ESV)

¹³ In him you also, when you heard the word of truth, the gospel of your salvation, and believed in him, were **sealed with the promised Holy Spirit**, ¹⁴ who is the guarantee of our inheritance until we acquire possession of it, to the praise of his glory.

Ephesians 2:18 English Standard Version (ESV)

¹⁸ For through him we both have **access in one Spirit** to the Father.

Ephesians 5:18 English Standard Version (ESV)

¹⁸ And do not get drunk with wine, for that is debauchery, but **be filled with the Spirit**,

1 Thessalonians 4:8 English Standard Version (ESV)

⁸ Therefore **whoever disregards** this, **disregards** not man but **God**, who **gives his Holy Spirit** to you.

Titus 3:5 English Standard Version (ESV)

⁵ **he saved us**, not because of works done by us in righteousness, but according to his own mercy, **by the washing of regeneration and renewal of the Holy Spirit**,

Hebrews 2:4 English Standard Version (ESV)

⁴ while God also bore witness **by signs** and **wonders** and various **miracles** and **by gifts of the Holy Spirit** distributed according to his will.

James 4:5 New American Standard Bible (NASB)

⁵ Or do you think that the Scripture speaks to no purpose: "He jealously desires **the Spirit which He has made to dwell in us**"?

1 John 2:20, 27 English Standard Version (ESV)

²⁰ But you have been **anointed by the Holy One**, and you all have knowledge.

²⁷ But **the anointing that you received from him abides in you**, and you have no need that anyone should teach you. But as his anointing teaches you about everything, and is true, and is no lie, just as it has taught you, abide in him.

1 John 4:13 English Standard Version (ESV)

¹³ By this we know that we abide in him and he in us, because **he has given us of his Spirit**.

The Holy Spirit and Today's Christians

Can The Holy Spirit do the same for us? No, the Holy Spirit cannot, at least not in the same way and the same sense. How, then, can we receive the Holy Spirit, to be instructed, guide, taught, reminded and to be directed in our witnessing to others in our evangelism work? As an aside, the answer will apply to every other facet of our Christian life as well, we just happen to be focusing on the evangelism aspect. Let us look at the thought of the Holy Spirit instructing and teaching Christians. Today we have over 41,000 different denominations, all teaching different doctrinal positions on the same subject matter. If we choose just one denomination, we find that each of the tens of thousands of pastors in the churches does not have to teach the same thing about the same doctrine. Then, let us take and one church within that denominations, and we will find that the church members do not all believe the same thing as their pastor.

Thus, we have all sorts of men teaching different views on every doctrine. Let us look at a few examples, so we can better understand. In dealing with inspiration of God's Word, most church leader teach The Infallibilist View, meaning that they believe the Bible is infallible only on matters of faith, but that it contains many mistakes, errors, and contradictions in matters when it touches on science, history, and geography. On the other hand, few conservative church leaders still teach The Inerrantist View, meaning that they believe the Bible is without error of any kind. On the doctrine of the atonement, some leaders have The Penal Substitution View, meaning that they believe that Christ died in our place. Others have the Christus Victor View, meaning that they believe Christ destroyed Satan and his works. While others have The Moral Government View, meaning that they believe Christ displayed God's wrath against sin. Concerning the doctrine of Sanctification, there are four main views. We have the Lutheran View, meaning sanctification as a declaration by God. We have the Calvinist view, meaning sanctification as holiness in Christ and personal conduct. Then, we have the Keswick View, meaning sanctification as resting-faith in the sufficiency of Christ. In addition, we have the Wesleyan, View, meaning entire sanctification as perfect love. Even these four beliefs on sanctification are not completely accepted because each church leader can tweak it to fit his understanding of things. These doctrines are just the beginning. We could cover The Providence Debate, i.e., the sovereignty of God. We could talk about different foreknowledge beliefs, the divine image differences the different salvation beliefs, the different beliefs about the human constitution, eternal security, the destiny of the evangelized, baptism, charismatic gifts, hellfire, and numerous others.

These differences in the Christian leader's beliefs are often contradictory. Are we to believe that the Holy Spirit one church leader to teach that sinners are destined to enteral torment in hellfire while other leaders teach eternal destruction for the sinners? Are we to believe that the Holy Spirit teaches different church leaders four different views on sanctification? The belief that the Holy Spirit is still carrying out the same work today as what the Father and the Son assigned in the first century, place the Holy Spirit in a very unenviable position, i.e., teaching different views on the same doctrine, some of which are even contradictory. Can we accept that the Holy Spirit teaches different views on all doctrinal positions, even being contradictory? Remember, it was the Holy Spirit, who taught and instructed the apostles miraculously. The Holy Spirit guided them as well. One way was in their writings, as no New Testament author contradicted another, they were all one because there was really one author, God. This is actually true of all forty plus authors of the entire Bible. Thus, we are to believe that the Holy Spirit moved over forty Bible authors miraculously, over a 1,600 year period, to pen sixty-six Bible books, in all of which there is not one contraction, error or mistake, but now the Holy Spirit is teaching different views and contradictory information? We would not say in the church of and leader, who taught contradictory information, so why would we accept that the Holy Spirit would do such a thing. Supposing that churches evangelized their own communities, which they do not, but let us suppose they did. How should an atheist feel if different churches came to his home to witness to him and they told him contradictory views about the same doctrine?

The problem is the belief that the Holy Spirit is carrying out the same work after that work was completed in the first century. Only the apostles and a select few fellow workers received the Holy Spirit in a direct and supernatural way, teaching them, guiding them, instructing them, bringing back to their remembrance all that Jesus had said. The apostle Paul told Timothy, "The things which you have heard from me in the presence of many witnesses, entrust these to faithful men who will be able to teach others also." (2 Tim. 2:2) We all know that Timothy traveled with Paul for 15 years, being taught by Paul (Paul already being extremely educated by Gamaliel), but more importantly, miraculously taught and instructed by the Holy Spirit. This clearly was not the case with Timothy (his being taught and instructed by the Holy Spirit in the same way and to the same extent), as Timothy was taught by Paul and his study of the Old Testament Scriptures. This text evidences that we are to be taught and instructed by Holy Spirit by way of our study the Holy, Spirit-inspired Scriptures.

If the Holy Spirit were miraculously teaching and instructing Christians today, as took place with the apostles and a select few fellow workers, there would be no need for any sort of Bible study tools, such as Bible dictionaries, encyclopedias, word study dictionaries, commentaries, and the like. Even so, while there are no direct Scriptures to evidence Timothy receiving Holy Spirit in the same way as Paul and the twelve apostles, we know that Holy Spirit led Paul to Timothy on his second missionary tour. We know that Paul saw something in Timothy that brought about a 15-year friendship and bond between the two like no other. Timothy became an extremely valuable co-worker of the apostle Paul, in a time, when the Holy Spirit was building the first century Christian congregation. Therefore, we cannot discount the possibility that Timothy was guided by the Holy Spirit as Paul had been, maybe not to the same degree, and that he was not taught and instructed in the same way and sense but used more directly by the Holy Spirit than those after the first century, including us today. Let us get back to the apostles for a moment. Let us look at the apostles in the very beginning of Acts, as Jesus tells them,

Acts 1:8 English Standard Version (ESV)

⁸ But you will receive power when the Holy Spirit has come upon you, and you will be my witnesses in Jerusalem and in all Judea and Samaria, and to the end of the earth."

Earlier, Jesus had told them that he was going away and that he was sending them a helper, the Holy Spirit. Now, he specifically tells them, "You [namely, the apostles] will receive power when the Holy Spirit has come upon you, and you will be my witnesses in Jerusalem and in all Judea and Samaria, and to the end of the earth." Just after Jesus said these things, as they were watching, he ascended back to heaven to be with the Father. Some days later on Sivan 6, 33 C.E., they would receive the power of the Holy Spirit, where there was an outpouring of Holy Spirit. (Acts 2:1-17, 38) If they had already received the Holy Spirit, they would not have needed to call the brothers together to determine who was going to replace Judas as the twelfth apostle. Moreover, "they cast lots for them [Joseph called Barsabbas, who was also called Justus, and Matthias], and the lot fell on Matthias, and he was numbered with the eleven apostles."– Acts 1:15-26

Obtain Boldness

Jesus told his listeners,

Luke 11:13 English Standard Version (ESV)

13 If you then, who are evil, know how to give good gifts to your children, how much

more will the heavenly Father give the Holy Spirit to those who ask him!"

If we want to receive the Holy Spirit, we just go to the Father in prayer and ask him. If want to be bolder in our sharing of the good news, we can pray to God for the Holy Spirit. However, we must not misunderstand the Scriptures, so as to expect the miraculous, supernatural gifts of the Holy Spirit in the same sense and the same way as the apostle, their fellow workers, and the Christians of the first century. If want to become a better teacher in the Bible class at our churches, we will have to be a better Bible student, take in many Scriptures that deal with the principles of being a more effective teacher, put these into practice, and maybe pick up some good Christian books on being a better teacher. In this way, we would be working in harmony with our prayer, because the Word of God is Spirit inspired, and thus the more we delve into it and apply it in a correct and balanced manner; in essence, we are getting more Holy Spirit. If we want to teach the Bible to the Spanish-speaking people in our community, we may want to learn the Spanish language.

Some might believe that I am suggesting that the Holy Spirit is not active today. This is not the case. It is not the question of whether the Spirit is active, but how the Spirit is active. We can all agree that the Holy Spirit is pleading with the unsaved world, to help them find the path of salvation that leads to accepting Jesus Christ. This is not accomplished in some miraculous, supernatural way, but rather through our work as ambassadors for Christ. New Testament Bible scholar Richard L. Pratt Jr., made the following comment on 1 Corinthians 5:20a,

> Paul's role in the divine plan of reconciliation led him to a remarkable claim. He and his company were **Christ's ambassadors**. "Ambassadors" was a technical political term used in Paul's day that closely parallels our English word "ambassadors." An ambassador represented a nation or kingdom in communication with other nations. Paul had in mind his apostolic call to represent the kingdom of Christ to the nations of the earth. Ambassadors held positions of great honor in the ancient world because they represented the authority of the kings on whose behalf they spoke.

> This was also true for Paul as the ambassador of Christ. When he spoke the message of reconciliation, it was **as**

though God were making his appeal through him. Rather than speaking directly to the nations of earth, God ordained that human spokespersons would speak for him. As an apostle, Paul had authority to lead and guide the church (2 Cor. 13:3, 10). Yet, this description applies to all who bear the gospel of Christ to others—even to those who do not bear apostolic authority (1 Pet. 4:11). Though we may not present the gospel as perfectly as Paul did, we do speak on God's behalf when we bring the message of grace to others. But Paul and his company were to be received as mouthpieces of God in the most authoritative sense. (Pratt Jr 2000, p. 359)

2 Corinthians 5:16-20 English Standard Version (ESV)

¹⁶ From now on, therefore, we regard no one according to the flesh. Even though we once regarded Christ according to the flesh, we regard him thus no longer. ¹⁷ Therefore, if anyone is in Christ, he is a new creation. The old has passed away; behold, the new has come. ¹⁸ All this is from God, who through Christ reconciled us to himself and gave us the ministry of reconciliation; ¹⁹ that is, in Christ

God was reconciling the world to himself, not counting their trespasses against them, and entrusting to us the message of reconciliation. 20 Therefore, we are ambassadors for Christ, God making his appeal through us. We implore you on behalf of Christ, be reconciled to God.

As ambassadors for Christ, we are not seeking to offer superficial feel-good solutions to the problems of their imperfection, nor the wicked world in which we live. We are not telling them that, if they accept Christ, God will take care of their problems, and they will feel better about life. Sadly, many who first come to a Christian meeting are looking for just that; they want God to help them cope with the imperfection that surrounds their every waking moment. We certainly can counsel them biblically, which will enable them to improve their lot in life, will help them be stronger in dealing with this imperfection we all face, and, generally speaking, if they live a Christlike life, there will be fewer problems that a worldly life. However, our serving as ambassadors for Christ, this is not the goal of our service to the unbelieving world. We are offering them the same gospel that Paul did. In other words, the Father loved the world of humankind so much, he offered the only begotten Son, and the

Father is willing to forgive any of their Adamic, inherited sin, by means of Christ Jesus. Paul wrote,

Romans 5:10-12, 32 English Standard Version (ESV)

[10] For if while we were enemies we were reconciled to God by the death of his Son, much more, now that we are reconciled, shall we be saved by his life. [11] More than that, we also rejoice in God through our Lord Jesus Christ, through whom we have now received reconciliation. [12] Therefore, just as sin came into the world through one man, and death through sin, and so death spread to all men because all sinned. [32] He who did not spare his own Son but gave him up for us all, how will he not also with him graciously give us all things?

APPENDIX A

APPENDIX A Does God Step in and Solve Our Every Problem Because We are Faithful?

Edward D. Andrews

Praising God as the Grand Savior

Psalm 42 depicts for us the circumstances of a Levite, one of the offspring's of Korah, who found himself in exile. His inspired words can be very beneficial to us in preserving thankfulness for friendship with fellow Christians and continuing steadfastly while going through hostile conditions.

Thirsting for God as a Deer Thirsts for Water

The psalmist stated,

Psalm 42:1-2 English Standard Version (ESV)

¹ As a deer pants for flowing streams,
  so pants my soul for you, O God.
² My soul thirsts for God,
  for the living God.
When shall I come and appear before God?

A female deer cannot survive long without water. If water is low, the deer will risk its life going out of cover to get at the lifesaving water, even though she knows that the prey could attack at any moment. Like the deer that longs for water because it is a matter of life or death, the psalmist longed for God. The word "pants" in the Hebrew means "to have a keen, consuming desire for." His driving passion was not for people, possessions, or prosperity but for God."[29]

The Bible lands are a dry country, where the vegetation wastes away rapidly throughout the dry season, and water is a very valuable commodity, as it is limited in the extreme. That is why the Psalmist says that he was a 'soul thirsting for God.' He had been going without his essential spiritual needs being satisfied, that is the freedom of going to the sanctuary;

---

[29] Anders, Max; Lawson, Steven (2004-01-01). *Holman Old Testament Commentary - Psalms: 11* (p. 224). B&H Publishing. Kindle Edition.

therefore, he asks when he might again "appear before God."

He had been confined because of persecution, which prevented him from having contact with his fellow believers, which resulted in intense sadness, unhappiness and hopelessness, as verse three indicates.

Psalm 42:3 English Standard Version (ESV)

³ My tears have been my food
   day and night,
while they say to me all the day long,
   "Where is your God?"

Because of this hostile situation, the Psalmist was depressed to the point of being unable to eat. Therefore, his 'tears were his food.' Yes, "day and night" tears would roll down his cheeks into his mouth. His isolation and distress were not enough, as his enemies aggravated his wounds by provoking, ridiculing, in a hurtful or mocking way, as they would say all day long, "Where is your God?" He needed to find a way to reassure himself during this time of difficulty, to not be overrun by sorrow and heartache.

Why am I in Despair?

Psalm 42:4-6 English Standard Version (ESV)

⁴ These things I remember,
    as I pour out my soul:
how I would go with the throng
    and lead them in procession to the house
of God
with glad shouts and songs of praise,
    a multitude keeping festival.

⁵ Why are you cast down, O my soul,
    and why are you in turmoil within me?
Hope in God; for I shall again praise him,
    my salvation ⁶ and my God.

My soul is cast down within me;
    therefore I remember you
from the land of Jordan and of Hermon,
    from Mount Mizar.

Here we find the Psalmist not living in the moment of suffering, but rather remembering a time before he was in exile. He 'pours out his soul,' reaching the depths of his inner self with such passion, as he reminisces within about the former days. The Levite recalls in his mind what life was like when he was in his land, as he lived and worshiped with his brother and sister Israelites, as they walked "to the house of God," to celebrate the festival. Initially, these memories did not bring joy, but the pain of knowing they were a thing of the past, deeply missed.

Then, he asked himself, "Why are you cast down, O my soul and why are you in turmoil within me"? At that moment, he realized that his hope of salvation was not in himself, but in God. Therefore, the sweet memories truly brought him relief! He knew that if he patiently waited, God would act in his behalf. He then knew that his unfavorable conditions were not going to define his faith that, in time God would aid him in his time of need. When that moment would happen, he would "praise him" for 'his salvation' and being 'his God.' He might have been far removed from the sanctuary, but the Psalmist kept his God at the forefront of his mind.

If we ever find ourselves in difficult times, unrelenting times, we need to follow the pattern set by the Psalmist. We need to remember that God is well aware of our circumstances, and he will not forsake us. We must realize that the issues that were raised by Satan in the Garden of Eden, the sovereignty of God, the rightfulness of his rulership, and the issues raised by Satan to God in the book of Job, the loyalty of God's creatures, are greater than we are.

Proverbs 3:25-26 Lexham English Bible (LEB)

²⁵ Do not be afraid of sudden panic,
    or the storm of wickedness that will
come.
²⁶ [Jehovah] will be your confidence
    and guard your foot from capture.

Before delving into the rest of Psalm 42, let us take a moment to establish what these verses do not mean. Should we understand that these verses or any others in Scripture teach that because we are wisely walking with God that he will miraculously step in to protect each servant personally from difficult times, diseases, mental disorders, injury or death? No. These sorts of miracles are the extreme exception to the rule. Of the 4,000 plus years of Bible history, from Adam to Jesus, with tens of millions of people living and dying, we have but a few dozen miracles that we know of in Scripture. Even in Bible times, miracles were not typical, far from it. Hundreds of years may pass with no historical record of a miracle happening at all.

If we are wisely walking with God, we can be confident that bodily disease, mental disorders, injury or early death is far less likely than if we were not. Moreover, we can draw on the resurrection hope. Does God miraculously move events to save us out of difficult times or miraculously heal us? Yes, he

128

certainly can, but it is an extreme exception to the rule. He miraculously heals those who are going to play a significant role in his settling of the issues that were raised in the Garden of Eden.

What God's Word teaches us is this, that if we walk by using discernment and exercising sound judgment from Scripture, unless unexpected events befall us, we can be sure that we will not stumble into the difficulties that the world of humankind alienated from God faces every day. Conversely, the wicked do not have this protection as they reject the Word of God as foolish. In other words, Christians live by the moral values of Scripture, which gives them an advantage over those who do not. Therefore, God answers our prayers by our faithfully acting in behalf of those prayers, by applying Scripture in a balanced manner. If we have not taken in a deep understanding of God's Word, how can we have the Spirit inspired wisdom, the very knowledge of God to guide and direct us in our ways? Just because we are not being rescued when we feel that we should, this does not mean that we have lost faith, or that God is displeased. Even though the Psalmist had no doubt that Jehovah God was coming to his aid, he still experienced grief.

Psalm 42:7 English Standard Version (ESV)

⁷ Deep calls to deep
    at the roar of your waterfalls;
all your breakers and your waves
    have gone over me.

Yes, the Psalmist's surroundings of his exile were very beautiful; however, they brought him back to the reality of his difficulty! Verse 7 may very well be describing the snow on Mount Hermon when it melts. Marvelous waterfalls are fashioned, which pour into the Jordan, causing it to increase in size. It is as though one wave is speaking to another wave. This extraordinary spectacle of power brought to the Psalmist's mind that he had been consumed by distress as if being overcome by a flood. Nevertheless, his faith in God does not waiver.

Psalm 42:8 English Standard Version (ESV)

⁸ By day [Jehovah]³⁰ commands his steadfast love,

---

³⁰ Translations take liberties with God's personal name, by removing it and replacing it with the title LORD in all caps. There is no rational reason, or Scriptural grounds for doing so. In fact, Scripture shows just the opposite.—See the American Standard Version Isaiah 42:8; Malachi 3:16; Micah 4:5; Proverbs

and at night his song is with me,
a prayer to the God of my life.

There is no doubt in the Psalmist's mind
that Jehovah God will engulf him with his
steadfast love, freeing him of anxiety. This will
empower him to praise God in song and to
offer a prayer of thanks 'to the God of his life.'

The Korahite Levite thinks,

Psalm 42:9-10 English Standard Version
(ESV)

[9] I say to God, my rock:
"Why have you forgotten me?
Why do I go mourning
because of the oppression of the enemy?"
[10] As with a deadly wound in my bones,
my adversaries taunt me,
while they say to me all the day long,
"Where is your God?"

Then, it seems that the Psalmist slips, even
though he views God as 'his rock,' a place of
protection from one's enemies. Yes, he now
asks, "Why have you forgotten me?" Yes, the
Psalmist was allowed to remain in his
circumstances of sadness, feeling depressed, as

18:10; Joel 2:32; Ezekiel 36:23; Exodus 9:16; Malachi
1:11; Psalm 8:1;148:3.

his enemies took pleasure in what appeared to be a victory. The psalmist speaks of himself as being criticized in an unbearable way. So malicious was the mockery and disdain that it could be likened 'as with a deadly wound in his bones.' However, the Levite again comes to himself with self-talk, challenging his irrational thinking with rational thinking.

Wait for God

Psalm 42:11 English Standard Version (ESV)

¹¹ Why are you cast down, O my soul,
    and why are you in turmoil within me?
Hope in God; for I shall again praise him,
    my salvation and my God.

It is not the troubles of the Psalmist, which actually caused him to feel bad. It is what he told himself that contributed to how he felt. Self-talk is what we tell ourselves in our thoughts. In fact, self-talk is the words we tell ourselves about people, self, experiences, life in general, God, the future, the past, the present; it is specifically all the words we say to ourselves all the time. Destructive self-talk, even subconsciously, can be very harmful to our mood: causing mood slumps, our self-worth plummeting, our body feeling sluggish, our will to accomplish even the smallest of things is not to be realized and our actions defeat us.

Intense negative thinking of the Psalmist led to his feeling forsaken, resulting in painful emotions, and depressive state. However, his thoughts based on a good mood were entirely different from those based on his being upset. Negative thoughts that flooded his mind were the actual contributors of his self-defeating emotions. These very thoughts were what kept the Psalmist sluggish and contributed to his feeling abandoned. Therefore, his thinking was also the key to his relief.

Every time the Psalmist felt down because of his irrational self-talk, he attempted to locate the corresponding negative thought he had to this feeling. It was those thoughts that created his feelings of low self-worth. By offsetting them and replacing them with rational thoughts, he actually changed his mood. The negative thoughts that move through his mind did so with no effort, and were the easiest course to follow, because imperfect human tendencies gave him that way of thinking, a pattern of thinking. However, the Psalmist challenged those irrational thoughts of being forsaken with rational ones, saying that he would hope in God and that he would continue to praise him as in the end God is his salvation, even if that salvation comes in the form of a resurrection.

The centerpiece to it all is our Christlike mind. Our moods, behaviors and body responses result from the way we view things (fleshly or spiritual). It is a proven fact that we cannot experience any event in any way, shape, or form unless we have processed it with our mind first. No event can depress us; it is our perception of that event that will contribute to intense sadness, even depression. If we are only sad over an event, our thoughts will be rational, but if we are depressed or anxious over an event, our thinking will be bent and irrational, distorted and utterly wrong.

If we are to remain rational in our thinking, we need to grasp the fact that God does not always step in when we believe he should, nor is he obligated to do so. As was stated earlier, he has greater issues that need resolving, which have eternal effects for the whole of humankind. There are far more times that when God does not step in, meaning that our relief may come in the hope of the resurrection. However, for his servants that apply his Word in a balanced manner, fully, God is acting in their best interest by way of his inspired, inerrant Word.

APPENDIX B

APPENDIX B Why Has God Permitted Suffering and Evil?

Edward D. Andrews

"God has morally sufficient reasons for permitting the evil and suffering in the world."—William Lane Craig

That morally sufficient reason lies below.

"The significant issue that drove me to Agnostcism [Bible Scholar Dr. Bart D. Ehrman is now an Agnostic] has to do not with the Bible, but with the pain and suffering in the world." He writes, "I eventually found it impossible to explain the evil so rampant among us—whether in terms of genocides (which continue), unspeakable human cruelty, war disease, hurricanes, tsunamis, mudslides, the starvation of millions of innocent children, you name it—if there was a good and loving God who was actively involved in this world." *Misquoting Jesus* (p. 248)

As you will see below, Ehrman's issue is simply a matter of starting with the wrong assumption. **Point One**: He starts with 'if God is a God of love, who has the power to fix anything, how can there have been such horrific pain and suffering in imperfection over the last 6,000 years?' **Point Two**: He also likely begins with the premise that 'God is responsible for everything that happens.' If one starts with the wrong assumption, there is no doubt that he will reach the wrong conclusion(s). **Point One** is dealt with below, but let it be said that Ehrman is looking through the binoculars from the opposite end, the big side through the small. When we do that, we get a narrow, focused outlook. God looks through the binoculars the correct way, and can see the big picture. Ehrman can only see but a fraction and a moment of time, 70 – 80 years, while God has seen everything that has happened over these past 6,000 plus years in the greatest of detail, and can see what the outcome would be if he had handled things in a variety of ways.

Point Two is certainly one reason suffering and evil is often misunderstood. God is responsible for everything, but not always directly. If he started the human race, and we end up with what we now have, in essence, he is responsible. Just as parents, who have a child are similarly responsible for the child committing murder 21 years into his life, because they procreated and gave birth to the child. The mother and father are indirectly responsible. King David commits adultery with

Bathsheba and has her husband Uriah killed to cover things up, and impregnates Bathsheba, but the adulterine child, who remains nameless, died. Is God responsible for the death of that child? We can answer yes and no to that question. He is responsible in two ways: **(1)** He created humankind, so there would have been no affair, murder, adulterine child if he had not. **(2)** He did not step in and save the child, when he had the power to do so. However, he is not directly responsible, because he did not make King David and Bathsheba commit the acts that led to the child being born, nor did he bring an illness on the adulterine child, he just did not move in to protect the child, in a time that had a high rate of infant deaths.

The reason people think that God does not care about us is the words of some religious leaders, which have made them, feel this way. When a tragedy strikes, what do some pastors and Bible scholars often say? When 9/11 took place, with thousands dying in the twin towers of New York, many ministers said: "It was God's will. God must have had some good reason for doing this." When religious leaders make such comments or similar ones, they are actually blaming God for the bad things that happened. Yet, the disciple James wrote, "Let no one say when he is tempted, 'I am being tempted by God,' for God cannot be tempted with evil, and he himself tempts no one." (James 1:13) God never directly causes what is bad. Indeed, "far be it from God that he should do wickedness, and from the Almighty that he should do wrong." Job 34:10.

The history of humans has been inundated with pain and suffering on an unprecedented scale, much of which they have brought on themselves. The problem/question that has plagued many persons is, 'why if there is a loving God, would he allow it to start with, and worse still, why allow it to go on for over 6,000 years?' Some apologist scholars have struggled to answer this question, because they are over analyzing, as opposed to just looking for the answer in God's Word. Therefore, if we are to answer this question, we must go back to Adam and Eve at the time of the first sin. Many have read this account, but I will list the texts as a refresher.

Genesis 2:17 English Standard Version (ESV)

[17] but of the tree of the knowledge of good and evil you shall not eat, for in the day that you eat of it <u>you shall surely die</u>."

As you can see, humankind's continued existence in a paradise, with perfection, was dependent upon obedience, his continued acceptance of God as his sovereign.

Genesis 3:1-5 English Standard Version (ESV)

[1] Now the serpent was more crafty than any other beast of the field that the LORD God had made. He said to the woman, "Did God actually say, 'You shall not eat of any tree in the garden'?" [2] And the woman said to the serpent, "We may eat of the fruit of the trees in the garden, [3] but God said, 'You shall not eat of the fruit of the tree that is in the midst of the garden, neither shall you touch it, lest you die.'" [4] But the serpent said to the woman, "<u>You will not surely die</u>. [5] For God knows that when you eat of it your eyes will be opened, and you will be like God, knowing good and evil."

Later Bible texts establish Satan the Devil as the one using a serpent as his mouthpiece, like a ventriloquist would a dummy. Anyway, take note that Satan contradicts the clear statement made to Adam at Genesis 2:17, "you will not surely die." Backing up a little, we see Satan asking an inferential question, "Did God actually say, 'You shall not eat of any tree in the garden'?" First, he is overstating what he knows to be true, not "any tree," just one tree. Second, Satan is inferring, 'I can't believe that

140

God would say . . . how dare he say such.' Notice too that Eve has been told so thoroughly about the tree that she even goes beyond what Adam told her, not just that you 'do not eat from it,' no, 'you do not even touch it!' Then, Satan out and out lied and slandered God as a liar, saying that 'they would not die.' To make matters much worse, he infers that God is withholding good from them, and by rebelling they would be better off, being like God, 'knowing good and bad.' This latter point is not knowledge of; it is the self-sovereignty of choosing good and bad for oneself, and act of rebellion for created creatures. What was symbolized by the tree is well expressed in a footnote on Genesis 2:17, in The Jerusalem Bible (1966):

> This knowledge is a privilege, which God reserves to himself and which man, by sinning, is to lay hands on, 3:5, 22. Hence it does not mean omniscience, which fallen man does not possess; nor is it moral discrimination, for unfallen man already had it and God could not refuse it to a rational being. It is the power of deciding for himself what is good and what is evil and of acting accordingly, a claim to complete moral

independence by which man refuses to recognize his status as a created being. The first sin was an attack on God's sovereignty, a sin of pride.

The Issues at Hand

(1) Satan called God a liar and said he was not to be trusted, as to the life or death issue.

(2) Satan's challenge, therefore, took into question the right and legitimacy of God's rightful place as the Universal Sovereign.

(3) Satan also suggested that people would remain obedient to God only as long as their submitting to God was to their benefit.

(4) Satan all but said that humankind was able to walk on his own, there being no need for dependence on God.

(5) Satan argued that man could be like God, choosing for himself what is right and wrong.

(6) Satan claimed that God's way of ruling was not in the best interests of humans, and they could do better without God.

Job 1:6-11 English Standard Version (ESV)

⁶ Now there was a day when the sons of God came to present themselves before the

LORD, and Satan also came among them. 7 The LORD said to Satan, "From where have you come?" Satan answered the LORD and said, "From(C) going to and fro on the earth, and from walking up and down on it." 8 And the LORD said to Satan, "Have you considered my servant Job, that there is none like him on the earth, a blameless and upright man, who fears God and turns away from evil?" 9 Then Satan answered the LORD and said, "<u>Does Job fear God for no reason</u>? 10 Have you not put a hedge around him and his house and all that he has, on every side? You have blessed the work of his hands, and his possessions have increased in the land. 11 But <u>stretch out your hand and touch all that he has, and he will curse you to your face</u>."

Job 2:4-5 English Standard Version (ESV)

4 Then Satan answered the LORD and said, "Skin for skin! All that <u>a man</u> has he will give for his life. 5 But stretch out your hand and touch his bone and his flesh, and he will curse you to your face."

This general reference to "a man," as opposed to explicitly naming Job, is suggesting that all men [and women] will only obey God when things are good, but when the slightest difficulty arises, he will not obey. If you were put to the test, would you prove your love for your heavenly Father and show that you preferred His rule to that of any other?

God Settles the Issues

There is one thing that Satan did not challenge, namely, the power of God. Satan did not suggest that God was unable to destroy him as an opposer. However, he did challenge God's way of ruling, not His right to rule. Therefore, it is a moral issue that must be settled.

An illustration of how God chose to deal with the issue can be demonstrated in human terms. A neighbor down the street slandered a man, who had a son and daughter. The slanderer said that he was not a good father, i.e., he withheld good from his children, and was so overbearing, to the point of being abusive. The slanderer stated that the children would be better off without the father. He further argued that the children had no real love for their father, and only obeyed him because of the food and shelter. How should the father deal with these false, slanderous accusations? If he were to go down the road and pummel the slanderer, it would only validate the lies, making the neighbors believe he is telling the truth.

The answer lies within his family as they can serve as his witnesses. (Pro 27:11; Isa 43:10) If the children stay obedient and grow to be successful adults, turning out to be loving, caring, honest people with spotless character, it proves the accusations false. If the children accept the lies and rebel, and grow up to be despicable people, it just further validates that they would have been better off by staying with the father. This is how God chose to deal with the issues. The issues that were raised must be settled beyond all reasonable doubt.

If God had destroyed the rebellious three: Satan, Adam and Eve; he would not have resolved the issues of

(1) whether man could walk on his own,

(2) if he would be better off without his Creator,

(3) if God's rulership were not best, and

(4) if God were hiding good from man.

(5) In addition, there was an audience of untold billions of angelic spirit creatures looking on.

If God destroyed without settling things, these spirit persons would be following God out of dreadful fear, not love, fear of displeasing God. Moreover, say He did kill them, and start over, and ten thousand years down the road (with billions of humans now on earth), the issues were raised again, He would have to destroy billions of people again, and again, and again all throughout time, until these issues were laid to rest.

What God has done is allow time to pass, and the issues to be resolved. Man thought he was better off without God, and could walk on his own. In addition, man has attempted every kind of rulership imaginable, and one must ask, 'have they proven themselves better than rulership under the sovereignty of their Creator?' (Proverbs 1:30-33; Isaiah 59:4, 8) Sadly, the issues must be taken up to the brink of destroying man (Rev. 11:18), otherwise, the argument would be that if given enough time, they could have turned things around. If man goes up to the point of destroying himself and Armageddon comes at the last minute, it will have set a case law, solved the issue, and the Bible can serve as the example forever. If the issues of God's sovereignty or the loyalty of His created creatures, angelic or human, is ever questioned again, we would have the Holy

Bible that will serve as a law established based on previous verdicts of not guilty, please see below.

What Have the Results Been?

(1) God does not cause evil and suffering. Romans 9:14.

(2) That fact that God has allowed evil, pain and suffering has shown that independence from God has not brought about a better world. Jeremiah 8:5, 6, 9.

(3) God's permission of evil, pain and suffering has also proved that Satan has not been able to turn all humans away from God. Exodus 9:16; 1 Samuel 12:22; Hebrews 12:1.

(4) The fact that God has permitted evil, pain and suffering to continue has provided proof that only God, the Creator, has the capability and the right to rule over humankind for their eternal blessing and happiness. Ecclesiastes 8:9.

(5) Satan has been the god of this world since the sin in Eden (over 6,000 years), and how has that worked out for man, and what has been the result of man's course of independence from God and his rule? Matthew

4:8-9; John 16:11; 2 Corinthians 4:3-4; 1 John 5:19; Psalm 127:1.

Satan's impact on the earth's activities has carried with it conflict, evil and death, and his rulership has been by means of deception, power and his own self-interest. He has demonstrated himself an unfit ruler of everything. Therefore, God is now completely vindicated in putting an end to this corrupted rebel along with all who have shared in his evil deeds. (Romans 16:20)

God has tolerated evil, sickness, pain, suffering and death until our day in order to resolve all the issues raised by Satan. We are self-centered in thinking that this has only pained us. Imagine that you are holding a rope on a sinking ship that 20 other men, women and children are clinging to, when your child loses her grip and falls into the ocean. You can either hold the rope, saving 20 people, or you can let go and attempt to rescue your daughter. God has been watching the suffering of billions from the day of Adam and Eve's sin. Moreover, it has been His great love for us, which causes Him to cling to the rope of issues, saving us from a future of repeated issues. Nevertheless, he will not allow this evil to remain forever. He has set a fixed time when He will end this wicked system of Satan's rule.

Daniel 11:27 Holman Christian Standard Bible (HCSB)

²⁷ The two kings, whose hearts are bent on evil, will speak lies at the same table but to no avail, for still the end will come <u>at the appointed time</u>.

Unlike what many people of the world may think (the world that lies in the hands of Satan), being obedient to God is not difficult. We simply must set our pride aside and accept that the wisdom of God is so far greater than our own, and accept that He has worked for the good of obedient humankind, as He loves each one of us.

Matthew 7:21 Holman Christian Standard Bible (HCSB)

²¹ "Not everyone who says to Me, 'Lord, Lord!' will enter the kingdom of heaven, but [only] the one who does the will of My Father in heaven.

1 John 2:15-17 Holman Christian Standard Bible (HCSB)

¹⁵ Do not love the world or the things that belong to the world. If anyone loves the world, love for the Father is not in him. Because everything that belongs to the world, ¹⁶ the lust of the flesh, the lust of the eyes, and the pride

in one's lifestyle, is not from the Father, but is from the world. [17]And the world with its lust is passing away, but the one who does God's will remains forever.

As Christians, there is a love we must not have. We must 'not love the world or anything in it.' Instead, we need to keep from becoming infected by the corruption of unrighteous human society that is alienated from God and must not breathe in its mental disposition or be moved by its sinful dominant attitude. (Ephesians 2:1, 2; James 1:27) If we were to have the views of those in the world that are in opposition to God, "the love of the Father" would not be in us. (James 4:4)

APPENDIX C Why Is Life So Unfair?

Edward D. Andrews

On December 14, 2012, 20-year-old Adam Lanza fatally shot twenty children and six adult staff members in a mass murder at Sandy Hook Elementary School, in the village of Sandy Hook in Newtown, Connecticut. Before driving to the school, Lanza shot and killed his mother Nancy at their Newtown home. As first responders arrived, he committed suicide by shooting himself in the head.[31]

Parents, who sent their children to school that morning, never expected that by the end of the day, Adam Lanza would have murdered them. Worse still, there were signs that, if paid attention to, things may have not turned out the way they did. These parents are certainly, what comes to mind when we think of life being unfair.

---

[31]http://en.wikipedia.org/wiki/Sandy_Hook_Element ary_School_shooting

Unfairness the World Over

The world is full of these type of accounts the world over. We have social depravities everywhere we look. In the United States, there are hundreds of thousands living in homeless shelters, under bridges, eating at soup kitchens, and many have young children with them as well. On the other hand, the United States throws away more food than any other country. Sadly, the hungry in the United States, while truly unfair, rates very low when one considers the inhumane conditions of other countries. In some countries, like Mexico, you have a millionaire living in a mansion, with a poor person living in a shack next door, and a person living in a car, living next door to him. Almost two billion people live in such hopeless poverty and inhuman conditions that those in the Western part of the world could never relate.

Poverty is defined as a state of want; lacking means; inadequacy. Poverty "brings hunger, disease, high infant mortality, homelessness, and even war." Poverty "falls on the more vulnerable groups in society, such as women, the elderly, minority groups, and children." About 1 billion people around the world live on less than $1 a day.[32]

God's View of Fairness

Leviticus 19:15 English Standard Version (ESV)

[15] "You shall do no injustice in court. You shall not be partial to the poor or defer to the great, but in righteousness shall you judge your neighbor.

Deuteronomy 32:4 English Standard Version (ESV)

[4] "The Rock, his work is perfect,
  for all his ways are justice.
A God of faithfulness and without iniquity,
  just and upright is he.

Acts 10:34-35 English Standard Version (ESV)

[34] So Peter opened his mouth and said: "Truly I understand that God shows no partiality, [35] but in every nation anyone who fears him and does what is right is acceptable to him.

---

[32] ttp://prezi.com/8duqy_es2rmu/inadequate-living-conditions-around-the-world/

From Where Does Unfairness Stem?

Genesis 2:17 Updated American Standard Version (UASV)

[17] "but from the tree of the knowledge of good and evil you shall not eat, for in the day that you eat from it you shall surely die."

Genesis 3:4-5 Updated American Standard Version (UASV)

[4] And the serpent **[Satan the Devil]** said to the woman, "You shall not surely die. [5] For God knows that when you eat of it your eyes will be opened, and you will be like God, knowing good and evil." knowing good and evil.

[6] So when the woman saw that the tree was good for food, and that it was a delight to the eyes, and that the tree was to be desirable to make one wise, and she took of its fruit and ate, then she also gave some to her husband when with her, and he ate.

Genesis 3:24 Updated American Standard Version (UASV)

[24] So he drove the man out, and at the east of the garden of Eden he placed the cherubim and a flaming sword that turned every way to guard the way to the tree of life.

John 8:44 English Standard Version (ESV)

⁴⁴ You are of your father the devil, and your will is to do your father's desires. He was a murderer from the beginning, and does not stand in the truth, because there is no truth in him. When he lies, he speaks out of his own character, for he is a liar and the father of lies.

Revelation 12:9 English Standard Version (ESV)

⁹ And the great dragon was thrown down, that ancient serpent, who is called the devil and Satan, the deceiver of the whole world, he was thrown down to the earth, and his angels were thrown down with him.

Unfairness in the Last Days

Revelation 12:12 English Standard Version (ESV)

¹² Therefore, rejoice, O heavens and you who dwell in them! But woe to you, O earth and sea, for the devil has come down to you in great wrath, because he knows that his time is short!"

Daniel 12:4 English Standard Version (ESV)

⁴ But you, Daniel, shut up the words and seal the book, until the time of the end. Many shall run to and fro, and knowledge shall increase."

2 Timothy 3:1-5 English Standard Version (ESV)

¹ But understand this, that in the last days there will come times of difficulty. ² For people will be lovers of self, lovers of money, proud, arrogant, abusive, disobedient to their parents, ungrateful, unholy, ³ heartless, unappeasable, slanderous, without self-control, brutal, not loving good, ⁴ treacherous, reckless, swollen with conceit, lovers of pleasure rather than lovers of God, ⁵ having the appearance of godliness, but denying its power. Avoid such people.

Unfairness Removed

Romans 16:20 English Standard Version (ESV)

20 The God of peace will soon crush Satan under your feet. The grace of our Lord Jesus Christ be with you.

Do Not Love the World

1 John 2:15-17 English Standard Version (ESV)

¹⁵ Do not love the world or the things in the world. If anyone loves the world, the love of the Father is not in him. ¹⁶ For all that is in the world, the desires of the flesh and the desires of the eyes and pride of life, is not from the Father but is from the world. ¹⁷ And the world is passing away along with its desires, but whoever does the will of God abides forever.

The End of the Age

Matthew 24:1-3 English Standard Version (ESV)

¹ Jesus left the temple and was going away, when his disciples came to point out to him the buildings of the temple. ² But he answered them, "You see all these, do you not? Truly, I say to you, there will not be left here one stone upon another that will not be thrown down." ³ As he sat on the Mount of Olives, the disciples came to him privately, saying, "Tell us, when will these things be, and what will be the sign of your coming and of the end of the age?"

Here in verse three, we have Jesus and the disciples taking a seat on the Mount of Olives, looking down on the temple below. The temple compound was the ninth wonder of the ancient world. Jesus had just told the disciples that this marvel was going to be so devastated in a coming destruction, "there will not be left here one stone upon another that will not be thrown down." Looking down, the disciples asked Jesus what they thought to be but one question, not knowing the answer that Jesus would give, showed it to be three separate questions. Of course, the initial question **(1)** was their wondering when the destruction that Jesus spoke of was coming. There second portion of that question was **(2)** what will be the sign of your coming. The third portion of the question was **(3)** the end of the age.[33] Herein, we will

---

[33] Whether one sees this as two questions or three questions is not that big of a difference. If it is two questions; then, the coming/presence of Christ and the end of the age are being treated as one event. However, if there are three; then, the coming/presence of Christ and the end of the age are being treated as two events. Either way, you have Christ's coming/presence and the end of the age. If the Greek word *parousia* carries the sense of both the arrival of Christ and his presence for a time before the end of the age, as explained by *Vine's Expository Dictionary*, this seems to better support it being a three part question. How long that interval is between the arrival, the presence and the conclusion, no one can truly know.

focus on questions **(2)** and **(3)**. In short, **(1)** the destruction of Jerusalem took place in 70 C.E., just 37-years after the death, resurrection, and ascension of Christ.

They ask these questions about the destruction of Jerusalem and the temple, his own second coming (... [*parousia*], presence, common in the papyri for the visit of the emperor), and the end of the world. Did they think that they were all to take place simultaneously? There is no way to answer. At any rate Jesus treats all three in this great eschatological discourse, the most difficult problem in the Synoptic Gospels. ... It is sufficient for our purpose to think of Jesus as using the destruction of the temple and of Jerusalem which did happen in that generation in a.d. 70, as also a symbol of his own second coming and of the end of the world (... [*sunteleias tou aiōnos*]) or consummation of the age. In a painting the artist by skilful perspective may give on the same surface the inside of a room, the fields outside the window, and the sky far beyond. Certainly in this discourse Jesus blends in apocalyptic language the background of his death on the cross, the coming destruction of Jerusalem, his own second coming and the end of the world. He now touches one, now the other. It is not easy for us to separate clearly the various items.[34]

In "what will be the sign of your **coming**," the Greek word behind "coming" (*parousia*) needs a little more in-depth explaining.

> *Parousia* ... lit., "a presence," *para*, "with," and *ousia*, "being" (from *eimi*, "to be"), denotes both an "arrival" and a consequent "presence with." For instance, in a papyrus letter a lady speaks of the necessity of her parousia in a place in order to attend to matters relating to her property there. Paul speaks of his *parousia* in Philippi, Phil. 2:12 (in contrast to his *apousia*, "his absence"; see absence). Other words denote "the arrival" (see *eisodos* and *eleusis*, above). *Parousia* is used to describe the presence of Christ with His disciples on the Mount of Transfiguration, 2 Pet. 1:16. When used

---

[34] A.T. Robertson, *Word Pictures in the New Testament* (Nashville, TN: Broadman Press, 1933), Mt 24:3.

of the return of Christ, at the rapture of the church, it signifies, not merely His momentary "coming" for His saints, but His presence with them from that moment until His revelation and manifestation to the world. In some passages the word gives prominence to the beginning of that period, the course of the period being implied, 1 Cor. 15:23; 1 Thess. 4:15; 5:23; 2 Thess. 2:1; Jas. 5:7-8; 2 Pet. 3:4. In some, the course is prominent, Matt. 24:3, 37; 1 Thess. 3:13; 1 John 2:28; in others the conclusion of the period, Matt. 24:27; 2 Thess. 2:8.[35]

"What will be the sign of your coming"
As we can see from the context of Matthew 24 and Vine's *Expository Dictionary*, parousia, describes not only the arrival of Christ, but his presence as well. This does not give us the sense of a coming and some swift departure. Rather,

---

[35] The reader should be aware that the Greek word parousia does mean presence, the word is derived from para (with) and ousia (being). However, it does not denote the idea of invisible as the Jehovah Witnesses attest to. See W. E. Vine, Merrill F. Unger, and William White Jr., *Vine's Complete Expository Dictionary of Old and New Testament Words* (Nashville, TN: T. Nelson, 1996), 111.

the presence aspect is a period of time that we cannot know the exact length of, so it does no good even to speculate by adding adjectives, like a "lengthy" or "short" presence.

"the end of the age" What is meant by the Greek word *aion*, which is translated "age." It refers to a certain period of time, an epoch, or age.

> *aion* (αἰών, 165), "an age, era" (to be connected with *aei*, "ever," rather than with *ao*, "to breathe"), signifies a period of indefinite duration, or time viewed in relation to what takes place in the period.[36]

What period of time is being referred to here? If we look at God's use of Moses to help in the Exodus of his people from Egypt, and Moses penning of the Mosaic Law, we would say that from the Exodus to the sacrifice ransom death of Christ was an "age" (period of time or epoch) where the Israelite nation was the only way to God. Then, Jesus entered humanity into another age by his ransom sacrifice, which runs

---

[36] W. E. Vine, Merrill F. Unger, and William White Jr., *Vine's Complete Expository Dictionary of Old and New Testament Words* (Nashville, TN: T. Nelson, 1996), 19.

up unto his second coming/presence and the end of this age of Christianity.

Jesus answers this two or three-part question throughout the rest of Matthew 24 and chapter 25. Matthew gives us Jesus' presentation of the events that lead to Jesus coming and presence, to set up his kingdom to rule **over** the earth for a thousand years. Most will be shocked by my saying "over" the earth, as almost all translations render Revelation 5:10 as "and you have made them a kingdom and priests to our God, and they shall reign **on** the earth."

> **epí** [2093] is in the genitive and can range from: "on, upon; over; at, by; before, in the presence of; when, under, at the time of;"[37] Below you are going to find a list of the genitive epi within Revelation that has a similar construction.
>
> If we are to establish that some translations are choosing a rendering because it suits their doctrine, we must compare how they render the same

---

[37] William D. Mounce, Mounce's Complete Expository Dictionary of Old & New Testament Words (Grand Rapids, MI: Zondervan, 2006), 1150.

thing elsewhere. I do believe that the English is a problem in trying to say, "They shall reign **on** the earth." First, because this is not a location issue: i.e., "where." The genitive *epi* is dealing not with where, but with authority over, which is expressed by having it over ... not on ...

Please also take special note that the context of all of these epi genitives that follow the active indicative verb and then are followed by the genitive definite article and noun are dealing with authority.

The verb "to reign" is properly used of kings and queens, and here implies complete power over the world and its inhabitants. So another way of expressing this is "and they shall rule over the world and its inhabitants" or "they shall have power over ...."[38]

Revelation 5:9-10 has a high level of theological content. It either says that Jesus and his co-rulers are going to over the earth, or on

---

[38] Bratcher, Robert G.; Hatton, Howard: A Handbook on the Revelation to John. New York: United Bible Societies, 1993 (UBS Handbook Series; Helps for Translators), S. 105

the earth. It is theological bias to have several cases of similar context and the same grammatical construction, rendering the verses the same every time, yet to then render one verse contrary to the others, simply because it aligns with one's theology. Please see Revelation 2:26; 6:8; 9:11; 11:6; 13:7; 14:18; 16:9; 17:18, and then look at Revelation **5:10**. Nowhere in Scripture does it say that Jesus is going to rule over the earth.

Signs of the End of the Age

Matthew 24:4 New American Standard Bible (NASB)

⁴ And Jesus answered and said to them, "See to it that no one misleads you.

Jesus' disciples, like any other Jew of the day, would have seen the destruction of Jerusalem in 70 C.E., the first century Jewish historian, Josephus, tells us 1,100,000 Jews were killed in the destruction of Jerusalem, with another 97,000 taken captive. (War VI. 9.3)[39] Therefore, here in advance (33 C.E.), Jesus wanted his disciples to be on the watch, to not

---

[39] Flavius Josephus and William Whiston, *The Works of Josephus: Complete and Unabridged* (Peabody: Hendrickson, 1987).

be misled, as though the destruction of Jerusalem (66-70 C.E.) also meant "the end of the age."

Matthew 24:5 English Standard Version (ESV)

⁵ For many will come in my name, saying, 'I am the Christ,' and they will lead many astray.

Yes, this would be one of the ways that many coming in Jesus' name would have led the disciples astray, claiming to be the Christ (Hebrew *Messiah*), namely the "anointed one." Therefore, it would not be Christians alone, who would be filling this role as false christs/messiahs/anointed ones.

"From Josephus it appears that in the first century before the destruction of the Temple [in 70 C.E.] a number of Messiahs arose promising relief from the Roman yoke, and finding ready followers ... Thus about 44, Josephus reports, a certain impostor, Theudas, who claimed to be a prophet, appeared and urged the people to follow him with their belongings to the Jordan, which he would divide for them. According to Acts v. 36 (which seems to refer to a different date), he secured about 400 followers. Cuspius

Fadus sent a troop of horsemen after him and his band, slew many of them, and took captive others, together with their leader, beheading the latter ... Another, an Egyptian, is said to have gathered together 30,000 adherents, whom he summoned to the Mount of Olives, opposite Jerusalem, promising that at his command the walls of Jerusalem would fall down, and that he and his followers would enter and possess themselves of the city. But Felix, the procurator (c. 55-60), met the throng with his soldiery. The prophet escaped, but those with him were killed or taken, and the multitude dispersed. Another, whom Josephus styles an impostor, promised the people "deliverance and freedom from their miseries" if they would follow him to the wilderness. Both leader and followers were killed by the troops of Festus, the procurator (60-62; "Ant." xx. 8, § 10). Even when Jerusalem was already in process of destruction by the Romans, a prophet, according to Josephus suborned by the defenders to keep the people from deserting announced that God commanded them to come to the Temple, there to receive miraculous signs of their deliverance. Those who came met death in the flames.

Unlike these Messiahs, who expected their people's deliverance to be achieved through divine intervention, Menahem, the son of Judas the Galilean and grandson of Hezekiah, the leader of the Zealots, who had troubled Herod, was a warrior. When the war broke out he attacked Masada with his band, armed his followers with the weapons stored there, and proceeded to Jerusalem, where he captured the fortress Antonia, overpowering the troops of Agrippa II. Emboldened by his success, he behaved as a king, and claimed the leadership of all the troops. Thereby he aroused the enmity of Eleazar, another Zealot leader, and met death as a result of a conspiracy against him (*ib.* ii. 17, § 9). He is probably identical with the Menahem b. Hezekiah mentioned in Sanh. 98b, and called, with reference to Lam. i. 17, "the comforter ["menaḥem"] that should relieve" (comp. Hamburger, "R. B. T." Supplement, iii. 80). With the destruction of the Temple the appearance of Messiahs ceased for a time. Sixty years later a politico-Messianic movement of large proportions took place with Bar Kokba at its head. This leader of the revolt against Rome was hailed as Messiah-king by Akiba, who referred to him. *The Jewish Encyclopedia* lists 28 false Messiahs between the years 132 C.E. and 1744 C.E.[40]

Matthew 24:6 English Standard Version (ESV)

⁶ And you will hear of wars and rumors of wars. See that you are not alarmed, for this must take place, but the end is not yet.

There have been religious leaders that have been misled by the two Great Wars of the 20th century, World War I and II, associating each of them with the "end of the age." The First Jewish–Roman War (66–73 C.E.),[41] at times

---

[40] Vol. X, pp. 252-255.

[41] The Second Jewish–Roman War (132–135 C.E.) Simon Bar Kokba, who claimed to be the long awaited Messiah, led a revolt against Roman Emperor Hadrian (76-139), for setting up a shrine to Jupiter (supreme Roman god), on the temple site in Jerusalem, as well as outlawing circumcision and instruction of the Law in public.

called The Great Revolt, could have misled the disciples into thinking that the end was imminent. Therefore, Jesus tells them that they should not be alarmed, and that the end is not yet. This counsel of Jesus has had to be applied from First Jewish–Roman War to the two Great Wars of the 20th century, every time a war came along, which seems to be an end all for humanity. Nevertheless, this one sign alone is not enough to signal the end, because imperfect humans are prone to war.

Matthew 24:7 English Standard Version (ESV)

⁷ For nation will rise against nation, and kingdom against kingdom, and there will be famines and earthquakes in various places.

Here Jesus expounds on his previous comments about war, because the conflicts of humankind have been so pervasive that there was a need for a reference book, *Dictionary of Wars* by George C. Kohn. Therefore, while we should take note of current events, wars, rumors of wars and even kingdom against kingdom is not enough alone to suppose that the end is here. Therefore, Jesus adds yet another two signs, famines and earthquakes. These two have been a part of humankind's history. Of course, the impact is going to be far greater with seven billion living people on earth, as opposed to a hundred million in 100 C.E. Nevertheless, these are just the beginning.

Matthew 24:8 English Standard Version (ESV)

⁸ All these are but the beginning of the birth pains.

Wars, rumors of wars, kingdoms again kingdom, famines and earthquakes are just the beginning of the things to come. However, they are not the goal post that the end is imminent. Such tragedies being merely a "beginning of the birth pains," the end was "not yet." Men likely cannot appreciate this verse, because the woman only knows the pain of giving birth to a child. It is the most natural thing in her life and yet the most painful. Therefore, consider that what comes after this metaphorical concept is going to be far more painful for humankind. These pains will grow in severity until the birth of the end of the age, and the return of Jesus. Nevertheless, like any other birth that has finally reached the end, the joy of a newborn child makes one forget the prior pains. This is true after the tribulation, the joys from the Kingdom will outweigh the previous pains.

Matthew 24:9 English Standard Version (ESV)

⁹ "Then they will deliver you up to tribulation and put you to death, and you will be hated by all nations for my name's sake.

Verse 9 of the new section, 9-12, begins with "then" (Greek *tote*), which brings the reader into another section of signs, offering us more of the lines in the fingerprint, the full picture that we are in the time of to the end. "Then" can have the meaning coming *after*, *or at the same time*, or it could mean simply *therefore*. It would seem that "then" is best understood as meaning 'at the same time,' because these signs, as well as those that we covered in 4-7, and those coming in verse 10 are of a composite sign. Meaning, you are looking for a time when they are all happening, and on a worldwide scale.

Who are "they" that deliver Christians up to tribulation? It would those Christians of verse 5, who were led astray, abandoning the Christian faith. The last 30 years, this has truly seen the abandonment of Christianity, as well as much tribulation for those that have remained faithful. What I am primarily referring to is liberal Christianity (80 percent of Christianity), who has abandoned the biblical truth, for the lie, so they can maintain a good relationship with the world, and progressivism. Christianity has never been more hated than it is today. Sadly, conservative Christians have been deeply opposed and persecuted by liberal Christianity, atheists, not to mention Islam and other religions.

Verse 9 says they will deliver you over (ESV), or hand you over (HCSB), to tribulation. If one is handed over, he must first be seized and then delivered to those, who are seeking to do him harm, even death. Why are the Christians hated so? Former Christians and liberal Christians hate the stand that conservative Christians take by truly living by God's Word, in a world that is anything but. Radical Islam is simply trying to impose themselves on everyone who stands in their way of dominating the world. Thus, being handed over is a result for one's true faith in Jesus Christ.

Matthew 24:10 English Standard Version (ESV)

10 And then many will fall away and betray one another and hate one another.

While early Christianity suffered horrible deaths through being martyred for simply being a Christian, the hatred today is just as vile by those that slaughter Christians around the world. Nevertheless, persecution through social media, news media, and by way of lawsuits, and protests in the streets, has become the new form of persecution in the Western world. Many have fallen away from Jesus, becoming apostates toward their former brothers and sisters, loathing their very existence.

Matthew 24:11 English Standard Version (ESV)

[11] And many false prophets will arise and lead many astray.

What is a prophet? The primary meaning is one who proclaims the word of God, a spokesperson for God. Therefore, a false prophet would be a spokesperson giving the impression that he is a spokesman for God, but really he is far from it. These ones are very subtle and deceptive in their ability to present themselves as a person representing God. Some modern day examples would be, Jim Bakker, Kenneth Copeland, Benny Hinn, T.D. Jakes, Joyce Meyer, Juanita Bynum, Creflo Dollar, Eddie Long, Pat Robertson, and Joel Olsteen. Of course, these are just some of the televangelists, who are false prophets, with tens of millions of followers. Other false prophet religious leaders have tens of millions of followers as well. Then, there are charismatic Christian denominations that numbered over 500 million followers. These ones claim gifts of

God (faith healing, speaking in tongues, etc.), which clearly are anything but. The true Christians are falling away in great numbers, being led astray by these false prophets, and those who have not, need to remain awake!

Matthew 24:12 English Standard Version (ESV)

[12] And because lawlessness will be increased, the love of many will grow cold.

The world we live in is overflowing with murders, rapes, armed robberies and assaults, not to mention war. It has grown so pervasive that many have grown callused to seeing the newspapers, websites and television news filled with one heinous crime, one after another. In looking at just one city in the United States, in 2012, 532 people were murdered in the city of Chicago, with a population of 2.7 million. However, in San Pedro Sula of the country Honduras, 1,143 people were murdered with only a population of 719,447. Statistics from the United Nations report 250,000 cases of rape or attempted rape annually. However, it must be kept in mind that because of the savagery of the times, in "many parts of the world, rape is very rarely reported, due to the extreme social stigma cast on women who have been raped, or the fear of being disowned by their families, or subjected to violence, including honor killings."[42]

Verse 12 says that the love of "the love of many will **grow cold**," and indeed it has. There are atrocious crimes against individuals, groups, nations, which would cripple the mind of anyone living decades ago. However, because of seeing it every day, all day long, the world has grown hardened to the lawlessness that exists around them. Christians carry the hope of salvation in their heart, which Jesus addresses next.

Matthew 24:13 English Standard Version (ESV)

[13] But the one who endures to the end will be saved.

What are we to endure? We are to endure while we maintain our walk with God through false Christs who will lead many astray, the wars, and the natural disasters. We are to endure while we maintain our walk with God through the loss of many of our spiritual brothers and sisters who fall away, the betrayal of former Christians, and the hatred of humankind who is alienated from God. We are to endure while we maintain our walk with

---

[42] http://en.wikipedia.org/wiki/Rape_statistics

God through false prophets that have arisen and lead many astray, the increase of the lawlessness in this world, and the love of humanity growing colder. Yes, each of us, who survives to the end of the Christian era, to the return of Christ, will be saved from Jesus' destruction of the wicked. However, we are not to simply sit around, we have a work to accomplish that is the last sign of the end of the age.

Matthew 24:14 English Standard Version (ESV)

[14] And this gospel of the kingdom will be proclaimed throughout the whole world as a testimony to all nations, and then the end will come.

This is the last of the signs that Jesus gave that should concern us, as it is directly related to the end of the age, and the return of Christ, namely '**the gospel of the kingdom being proclaimed throughout the whole world**.' Jesus makes it very clear what he meant by "the whole world," by then saying "all nations" (Gk., *ethnos*). What Jesus meant here was more directed toward all races, not so much the "nations" that we know the world to be divided into today. Therefore, Jesus speaking of the whole world was a reference to "**a body of** persons united by kinship, culture, and common traditions, *nation, people*."[43] Today, while for the most part, nations are made up of different races, the world is also becoming a melting pot.

In the phrase "**testimony** to all nations," we find the Greek word *martyrion*, which was a legal term of "**that which serves as testimony or proof,** *testimony, proof*."[44] The testimony here that is to be shared by Christ's disciples has to with Jesus and the kingdom. Evidence, proof, testimony has the ability to overcome the false reasoning of those in the world, to win them over, as well as convict those who refuse to see the evidence for what it is. Elsewhere Jesus said very clearly,

Matthew 11:15 (ESV)	**Matthew 13:9** (ESV)	**Matthew 13:43** (ESV)
[15] He who has ears to hear, let him hear.	[9] He who has ears, let him hear."	[43] Then the righteous will shine like the sun in the kingdom of

---

[43] William Arndt, Frederick W. Danker, and Walter Bauer, *A Greek-English Lexicon of the New Testament and Other Early Christian Literature* (Chicago: University of Chicago Press, 2000), 276.

[44] IBID, 619.

		their Father. He who has ears, let him hear.

No One Knows That Day and Hour

Matthew 24:36 English Standard Version (ESV)

[36] "But concerning that day and hour no one knows, not even the angels of heaven, nor the Son, but the Father only.

While none of us can know the precise time of Jesus' return, we do know that we are to be busy in the work that he has given us. Regardless of the time left, how will you use it? Here is how we should use our time before Christ's return. We should **live as though it is tomorrow**, but **plan as though it is 50-years away**. What do we mean by this? We live as though Christ is returning tomorrow, by walking with God, having a righteous standing before him. We plan as though it is 50-years away by living a life that makes strategies for a long-term evangelism that fulfills our end of the great commission. (Matt 24:14; 28:19-20; Ac 1:8)

Our sinful nature would not do well if we knew the exact day and hour. We do badly enough when we simply think Christ's return is close. You have had religions that have set dates for Christ's return, or are constantly saying, 'the end is near!' The ones who set actual dates for Christ's return: quit their jobs, sell their homes, take all their money out of the bank, and take their kids out of school, either (1) to have a good time before the end, or (2) to spend the last couple years yelling from the rooftops that "the end is coming!"

Those who are constantly saying, 'the end is near,' are similar, in that they do not take job promotions, because it would cut into their evangelism, they do not allow their children to have university educations or plan careers, because to them the end is near. Nevertheless, these groups are at least concerned about their evangelism, but fail to realize, we do not know when the end is coming.

We need to find a way in the time that remains, be it 5 years, 50 years, or 500 years, to encourage and foster "sincere brotherly love," and to display "obedience to the truth." What do we need to be obedient to? **(1)** We need to clean up the household of Christianity. **(2)** We need to then, carry out the great commission that Jesus assigned, to preach, to teach, and to make disciples! (Matt 24:14; 28:19-20; Ac 1:8) It is our assignment, in the time remaining, to assist God in helping those with a receptive heart, to accept the good news of the kingdom. Yes, we are offering those of the world, the hope of getting on the path of salvation, an opportunity at everlasting life. Just because we do not know the day or the hour, does not mean that we should be less urgent about this assignment. Remember Jesus' illustration,

Matthew 24:43 English Standard Version (ESV)

43 But know this, that if the master of the house had known in what part of the night the thief was coming, he would have stayed awake and would not have let his house be broken into.

Moreover, remember Jesus' question,

Luke 18:8 English Standard Version (ESV)

8 I tell you, he will give justice to them speedily. Nevertheless, when the Son of Man comes, will he find faith on earth?"

If we were to consider the chaos within Christianity today, the 41,000 different denominations of Christianity, all believing differently, could we honestly say that Jesus would truly find the faith?

Fairness Restored

Isaiah 2:1-4 English Standard Version (ESV)

¹ The word that Isaiah the son of Amoz saw concerning Judah and Jerusalem.

² It shall come to pass in the latter days
  that the mountain of the house of the Lord
shall be established as the highest of the mountains,
  and shall be lifted up above the hills;
and all the nations shall flow to it,
³   and many peoples shall come, and say:
"Come, let us go up to the mountain of
the Lord,
  to the house of the God of Jacob,
that he may teach us his ways
  and that we may walk in his paths."
For out of Zion shall go the law,
  and the word of the Lord from Jerusalem.
⁴ He shall judge between the nations,
  and shall decide disputes for many peoples;
and they shall beat their swords into
plowshares,
  and their spears into pruning hooks;
nation shall not lift up sword against nation,
  neither shall they learn war anymore.

On these verses, Trent C. Butler writes, "**2:1**. This section begins with another introduction much like Isaiah 1:1, but this one only introduces the following sermons, not the entire book. What follows is a vision, what Isaiah ... saw. Interestingly, the first part of this vision also appears in Micah 4:1–5. The form of this sermon sounds like a call to worship introduced by a prophetic announcement of salvation. Apparently Isaiah and his younger contemporary Micah both used the same call to worship from the Jerusalem temple to speak to God's people. This would mean that God used the temple hymnody as a source for his inspired word."

"2:2. While the destruction of Jerusalem dominated chapter 1, the city's function as the center of salvation for all nations introduces this section. The last days are still within world history with separate nations acting. Israel used the same language as her Near Eastern neighbors in talking about the national temple as the highest mountain on earth where the deity fights battles for his people (cp. Pss. 46; 48). The prophet Isaiah applied this language to the temple in Jerusalem even though Jerusalem was obviously not the highest of the mountains Israel could see. Jerusalem would be high and lifted up because God was at work there, causing his purpose for the world to be realized in historical events. The emphasis is not on the height of Jerusalem. The emphasis is on the unheard-of foreign nations coming to Jerusalem to worship. God's hope always encompasses the world, not just one small nation (see Gen. 12:1–4)."

"**2:3–4**. The prophet, as he often did, took up the popular theology of the people's hymnody and subtly shifted it from present to future tense. Only in the last days would Zion occupy such an exalted position. God would no longer battle the nations. Jerusalem could no longer glory in the hope that nations would march to her with large gifts and tribute for her victorious king. The prophetic hope is that God's word will become the world's weapon. Military academies and weapons will vanish. People will learn to live according to God's ways. They will obey his teachings. Nations will come to Jerusalem, not because a victorious king forces them to, but because they are attracted to Jerusalem by the God who lives there and the wisdom he gives there. No longer will they have to fight to settle their differences. In Jerusalem God will be the great Mediator who settles all human disputes without battle. Military weapons will become obsolete. The world's only war will be on poverty and hunger."[45]

Isaiah 11:3-5 English Standard Version (ESV)

[3] And his delight shall be in the fear of the Lord.
He shall not judge by what his eyes see,
   or decide disputes by what his ears hear,
[4] but with righteousness he shall judge the poor,
   and decide with equity for the meek of the earth;
and he shall strike the earth with the rod of his mouth,
   and with the breath of his lips he shall kill the wicked.
[5] Righteousness shall be the belt of his waist,
   and faithfulness the belt of his loins.

On these verses, Trent C. Butler writes, "The wise king would enter the royal courtroom to judge his nation correctly. As judge, the king would be empowered with the breath of his lips, the same word translated "Spirit" in verse 2. By this he would protect the poor from the wicked, establishing the economic justice so central to prophetic

---

[45] Anders, Max; Butler, Trent (2002-04-01). Holman Old Testament Commentary - Isaiah (p. 29-30). B&H Publishing.

185

preaching. The new age established by the new king would bring righteousness, a dominant theme for Isaiah. Coupled with faithfulness, this clothed the king for his royal reign."[46]

Isaiah 42:1 English Standard Version (ESV)

[42] Behold my servant, whom I uphold,
my chosen, in whom my soul delights;
I have put my Spirit upon him;
he will bring forth justice to the nations.

On this verse, Trent C. Butler writes, "This is the first of four "Servant Songs" in Isaiah 40-55 (49:1–6; 50:4–9; 52:13–53:12). Here God formally presented the servant to an audience, although both the name of the servant and the nature of the audience remain mysteriously unclear. We do not have to find answers to all our questions about the servant. We need to understand that he is God's chosen one, God takes great delight in him, and God upholds or supports him."

"The servant's mission surprised Israel and it surprises us. His mission was not to deliver Israel from captivity and exile. The mission was for the nations. The servant gained power for

---

[46] Anders, Max; Butler, Trent (2002-04-01). Holman Old Testament Commentary - Isaiah (p. 83). B&H Publishing.

his mission from the divine Spirit just as earlier rulers and prophets had. (For Spirit of God, see "Deeper Discoveries," chs. 62-64.) The servant's task was to bring justice to the nations. (For justice, see "Deeper Discoveries," ch. 1.) Justice involves a much broader meaning than the English term. In verse 4 it stands parallel to Torah, law or teaching. It is the verdict handed down by a judge (2 Kgs. 25:6); the whole court process (Isa. 3:14); the gracious and merciful judgment of God (Isa. 30:18); or the natural right and order claimed by a person or group of persons (Exod. 23:6)."

"In our text, the term for the servant's mission apparently encompasses a broad meaning. It refers to the natural world order and the rights expected by the nations of the earth within that order. God restores that order with its natural rights through his gracious and merciful judgment on the basis of his law or teaching."[47]

Isaiah 35:3-7 English Standard Version (ESV)

---

[47] Anders, Max; Butler, Trent (2002-04-01). Holman Old Testament Commentary - Isaiah (p. 232). B&H Publishing.

³ Strengthen the weak hands,
   and make firm the feeble knees.
⁴ Say to those who have an anxious heart,
   "Be strong; fear not!
Behold, your God
   will come with vengeance,
with the recompense of God.
   He will come and save you."

   ⁵ Then the eyes of the blind shall be
opened,
   and the ears of the deaf unstopped;
⁶ then shall the lame man leap like a deer,
   and the tongue of the mute sing for joy.
For waters break forth in the wilderness,
   and streams in the desert;
⁷ the burning sand shall become a pool,
   and the thirsty ground springs of water;
in the haunt of jackals, where they lie down,
   the grass shall become reeds and rushes.

On these verses, Trent C. Butler writes, "The revelation of God's glory provided the background for a new prophetic commission (vv. 3-4; cp. ch. 6). If God could change the dry wasteland so radically, how much more he could do so for humanity! The prophet was called to encourage the weak and feeble. Their reason for fear would vanish. God would come in vengeance. The divine appearance would destroy the enemy (34:8) but bring salvation to the people of God. Such salvation is not limited to a spiritual realm. The sick and disabled would find all their reasons for having an inferiority complex destroyed."[48]

Isaiah 65:20-23 English Standard Version (ESV)

20 No more shall there be in it
 an infant who lives but a few days,
 or an old man who does not fill out his days,
for the young man shall die a hundred years old,
 and the sinner a hundred years old shall be accursed.
21 They shall build houses and inhabit them;
 they shall plant vineyards and eat their fruit.
22 They shall not build and another inhabit;
 they shall not plant and another eat;
for like the days of a tree shall the days of my people be,
 and my chosen shall long enjoy the work of their hands.
23 They shall not labor in vain
 or bear children for calamity,
for they shall be the offspring of the blessed of

---

[48] Anders, Max; Butler, Trent (2002-04-01). Holman Old Testament Commentary - Isaiah (p. 191). B&H Publishing.

the Lord,
and their descendants with them.

On these verses, Trent C. Butler writes, "The injustices of life would disappear. Long life would be the rule for God's people, death at a hundred being like an infant's death that could only be explained as the death of a sinner. All of God's people would live to a ripe old age and enjoy the fruits of their life. The age of Messiah would clearly have dawned (cp. 11:6–9). No longer would people lose their property and crops to foreign invaders. Each of God's faithful people would enjoy the works of their hands. Labor would be rewarded in the field and in the birth place. Every newborn would escape the "horror of sudden disaster" (author's translation; NIV, misfortune). Curses would disappear. Every generation would be blessed by God."[49]

Psalm 37:7-11 English Standard Version (ESV)

[7] Be still before the Lord and wait patiently for him;
fret not yourself over the one who prospers

---

[49] Anders, Max; Butler, Trent (2002-04-01). Holman Old Testament Commentary - Isaiah (p. 374). B&H Publishing.

in his way,
  over the man who carries out evil devices!

  8 Refrain from anger, and forsake wrath!
  Fret not yourself; it tends only to evil.
9 For the evildoers shall be cut off,
  but those who wait for the Lord shall inherit
the land.

  10 In just a little while, the wicked will be no
more;
  though you look carefully at his place, he
will not be there.
11 But the meek shall inherit the land
  and delight themselves in abundant peace.

On these verses, Stephen J. Lawson wrote, "David repeated his original advice: Do not fret when men succeed. He returned to the earlier thought of verse 2—sinners who seem to flourish for a season will eventually be destroyed (Eccl. 3:16–17). To point this out, he used a series of contrasts between the godly and the ungodly. **Refrain from anger**, he declared, because these **evil men** in the final day would be cut off and die before entering eternity damned. **But those who hope in the LORD**—the meek—**will inherit the land** (cp.

Matt. 5:5). This indicated the fullness of God's blessing."[50]

Revelation 21:3-4 English Standard Version (ESV)

³ And I heard a loud voice from the throne saying, "Behold, the dwelling place of God is with man. He will dwell with them, and they will be his people, and God himself will be with them as their God. ⁴ He will wipe away every tear from their eyes, and death shall be no more, neither shall there be mourning, nor crying, nor pain anymore, for the former things have passed away."

On these verses, Kendell Easley wrote, "For the third and final time John hears **a loud voice from the throne** (16:17; 19:5). The word for **dwelling** is traditionally translated "tabernacle" or "tent." When the Israelites had lived in the wilderness after the exodus, God's presence was evident through the tent (Exod. 40:34). Part of the reward for Israel's obedience to God was, "I will put my dwelling place [tabernacle] among you, and I will not abhor you. I will walk among you and

---

50 Anders, Max; Lawson, Steven (2004-01-01). Holman Old Testament Commentary - Psalms: 11 (p. 199). B&H Publishing.

be your God, and you will be my people" (Lev. 26:11–12). Israel's disobedience, of course, led finally to the destruction of the temple."

"The permanent remedy began when God became enfleshed in Jesus: "The Word became flesh and made his dwelling among us" (John 1:14). A form of the same verb translated "made his dwelling" in John 1:14 is now used by the heavenly voice: **he will live with them**. Here, then, is the final eternal fulfillment of Leviticus 26."

"They will be his people, and God himself will be with them and be their God is a divine promise often made, particularly in context of the new covenant (Jer. 31:33; 32:38; Ezek. 37:27; 2 Cor. 6:16). In eternity, it will find full completion in its most glorious sense. One striking note here is that the word translated "people," while often singular in Revelation (for example, 18:4), here is plural, literally "peoples." This points to the great ethnic diversity of those in heaven."

"The great multitude who came out of the Great Tribulation received the pledge of many blessings including the final removal of any cause for **tears** (7:15–17). Now this promise extends to every citizen-saint of the New Jerusalem. The picture of God himself gently taking a handkerchief and wiping away all tears is overwhelming. It pictures the removal of four more enemies:

• **death**—destroyed and sent to the fiery lake (20:14; 1 Cor. 15:26)

• **mourning**—caused by death and sin, but also ironically the eternal experience of those who loved the prostitute (18:8)

• **crying**—one result of the prostitute's cruelty to the saints (18:24)

• **pain**—the first penalty inflicted on mankind at the Fall is finally lifted at last (Gen. 3:16)"

"All these belonged to **the old order of things** where sin and death were present. The last thought could also be translated, "The former things are gone." No greater statement of the end of one kind of existence and the beginning of a new one can be found in Scripture." (Easley 1998, p. 395)

Resurrection of Life and Judgment

John 5:28-29 English Standard Version (ESV)

[28] Do not marvel at this, for an hour is coming when all who are in the tombs will hear

his voice ²⁹ and come out, those who have done good to the resurrection of life, and those who have done evil to the resurrection of judgment.

When Jesus returns, he will bring many angels, and wipe out the wicked. However, the righteous will not be destroyed, and the righteous prior to Jesus first coming back in the first century, will receive a resurrection. The unrighteous, which had never had the opportunity to know God, will also be resurrected for a chance to hear the Good News, and then, they will be judged on what they do during the millennial reign of Christ. Acts 24:15) Therefore, the punishment for sin is death, the punishment for those, who "keep on sinning deliberately after receiving the knowledge of the truth, there no longer remains a sacrifice for sins," i.e., eternal death. However, "there will be a resurrection of both the just and the unjust [i.e., those who never heard the Good News]."--Acts 24:15

In death, Scripture show us as being unable to praise God. The Psalmist tells us, "For in death there is no remembrance of you; in Sheol [gravedom] who will give you praise?" (Psa. 6:5) Isaiah the prophet writes, "For Sheol [gravedom] cannot thank you [God], death cannot praise you; those who go down to the pit cannot hope for your faithfulness. 'It is the living who give thanks to you, as I do today; a father tells his sons about your faithfulness.'" (Isa 38:18-19)

Passing Over from Death to Life

John 5:24 English Standard Version (ESV)

[24] Truly, truly, I say to you, whoever hears my word and believes him who sent me has eternal life. He does not come into judgment, but has passed from death to life.

Regeneration is God restoring and renewing somebody morally or spiritually, where the Christian receives a new quality of life. This one goes from the road of death over to the path of life. (John 5:24) Here he becomes a new person, with a new personality, having removed the old person. (Eph. 4:20-24) **This does not mean** that the imperfection is gone, and the sinful desires are removed, but that he now has the mind of Christ, the Spirit and the Word of God to gain control over his thinking and his fleshly desires. Therefore, if one has truly experienced a conversion it will be evident by the changes in one's new personality from the old personality, his life, and his actions. If this is the case, he will be fulfilling the words of Jesus, "let your light shine before others, so that they may see your good works and give glory to your Father who is in heaven." (Matt. 5:16)

Can we see one as truly a man of faith, a committed Christian, who attends the meetings, but never carries out any personal study, never shares the gospel with another, never helps his spiritual brothers or sisters (physically, materially, mentally, or spiritually), nor helps his neighbor, or any of the other things one would find within a man of faith? James had something to say about this back in chapter 1:26-27, "If anyone thinks he is religious and does not bridle his tongue but deceives his heart, this person's religion is worthless. Religion that is pure and undefiled before God, the Father, is this: to visit orphans and widows in their affliction, and to keep oneself unstained from the world." One who does not possess real faith, will not help the poor, he will not separate himself from worldly pursuits, he will favor those that he can benefit from (the powerful and wealthy), and ignore those than he cannot make gains from (orphans and widows), he will not know the love of God, nor his mercy. (Jas. 2:8, 9, 13)

Titus 3:5 Lexham English Bible (LEB)

[5] he saved us, not by deeds of righteousness that we have done, but because of his mercy, **through the washing of regeneration** and renewal by the Holy Spirit,

The Greek word *polingenesia* means to a renewal or rebirth of a new life in Christ, by the Holy Spirit. Jesus told Nicodemus, "unless someone is born of ... Spirit, he is not able to enter into the kingdom of God." (John 3:5). At the moment a person is converted, he is regenerated or renewed, passing over from death to life eternal. Jesus explains this at John 5:24, "the one who hears my word and who believes the one who sent me has eternal life, and does not come into judgment, but has passed from death into life." The principal feature of rebirth of a new life in Christ, by the Holy Spirit, regeneration, is the passing over from death to life eternal.

At that point, the Spirit dwells within this newly regenerated one. From the time of Adam and Eve, God has desired to dwell with man. God fellowshiped with Adam in the Garden of Eden. After Adam's rebellion, he chose faithful men, to walk with him in their life course, to communicate with them. Enoch, Noah, and Abraham walked with God. In the Hebrew language the tabernacle is called *mishkan* meaning "dwelling place." In both the tabernacle and the temple, God was represented as dwelling with the people in the Most Holy. He also dwelt with the people through the Son, "And the Word became flesh and dwelt among us, and we have seen his glory, glory as of the only Son from the Father, full of grace and truth." (John 1:14) After Jesus' ascension, God dwelt among the Christians, by way of the Holy Spirit, in the body of each individual Christian, which begins at conversion.

Bibliography

Akin, Daniel L., David P. Nelson, and Jr. Peter R. Schemm. *A Theology for the Church*. Nashville: B & H Publishing, 2007.

Anders, Max. *Holman New Testament Commentary: vol. 8, Galatians, Ephesians, Philippians, Colossians*. Nashville, TN: Broadman & Holman Publishers, 1999.

Anders, Max, and Trent Butler. *Holman Old Testament Commentary: Isaiah*. Nashiville, TN: B&H Publishing, 2002.

Bercot, David W. *A Dictionary of Early Christian Beliefs*. Peabody: Hendrickson, 1998.

Blomberg, Craig. *The New American Commentary: Matthew*. Nashville, TN: Broadman & Holman Publishers, 1992.

Boa, Kenneth, and Kruidenier. *Holman New Testament Commentary: Romans*. Nashville: Broadman & Holman, 2000.

Borchert, Gerald L. *The New American Commentary: John 1-11* . Nashville, TN: Broadman & Holman Publishers, 2001.

Borchert, Gerald L. *The New American Commentary vol. 25B, John 12–21*.

Nashville: Broadman & Holman Publishers, 2002.

Brand, Chad, Charles Draper, and England Archie. *Holman Illustrated Bible Dictionary: Revised, Updated and Expanded.* Nashville, TN: Holman, 2003.

Bromiley, Geoffrey W., and Gerhard Friedrich. *Theological Dictionary of the New Testament, ed. Gerhard Kittel, vol. 4.* Grand Rapids, MI: Eerdmans, 1964-.

Campbell, Alexander. *The Christian System (6th ed.;.* Cincinnati: Standard, 1850.

Easley, Kendell H. *Holman New Testament Commentary, vol. 12, Revelation.* (Nashville, TN: Broadman & Holman Publishers, 1998.

Easton, M. G. *Easton's Bible Dictionary.* Oak Harbor, WA: Logos Research Systems, 1996, c1897.

Elwell, Walter A. *Evangelical Dictionary of Theology (Second Edition).* Grand Rapids: Baker Academic, 2001.

Elwell, Walter A, and Philip Wesley Comfort. *Tyndale Bible Dictionary.* Wheaton, Ill: Tyndale House Publishers, 2001.

Enns, Paul P. *The Moody Handbook of Theology.* Chicago: Moody Press, 1997.

Erickson, Milliard J. *Christian Theology (Third Edition).* Grand Rapids, MI: Baker Academic, 2013.

Ferguson, Everett. *Baptism in the Early Church: History, Theology, and Liturgy in the First Five Centuries .* Grand Rapids, MI: Eerdmans, 2009.

Gangel, Kenneth O. *Holman New Testament Commentary: Acts.* Nashville, TN: Broadman & Holman Publishers, 1998.

Gangel, Kenneth O. *Holman New Testament Commentary, vol. 4, John .* Nashville, TN: Broadman & Holman Publishers, 2000.

Geisler, Norman L. *SYSTEMATIC THEOLOGY: God and Creation (Vol. 2).* Minneapolis: Baker Publishing Group, 2003.

George, Timothy. *The New American Commentary: Galatians .* Nashville, TN: Broadman & Holman Publishers, 2001.

Green, Joel B, Scot McKnight, and Howard Marshall. *Dictionary of Jesus and the Gospels.* Downers Grove, IL: InterVarsity Press, 1992.

Gruden, Wayne. *Are Miraculous Gifts for Today?: 4 Views (Counterpoints: Bible and Theology)*. Grand Rapids: Zondervan, 2011.

Larson, Knute. *Holman New Testament Commentary, vol. 9, I & II Thessalonians, I & II Timothy, Titus, Philemon*. Nashville, TN: Broadman & Holman Publishers, 2000.

Lea, Thomas D. *Holman New Testament Commentary: Vol. 10, Hebrews, James*. Nashville, TN: Broadman & Holman Publishers, 1999.

Lea, Thomas D., and Hayne P. Griffin. *The New American Commentary, vol. 34, 1, 2 Timothy, Titus*. Nashville: Broadman & Holman Publishers, 1992.

Martin, D Michael. *The New American Commentary 33 1, 2 Thessalonians*. Nashville, TN: Broadman & Holman, 2001, c1995.

Mcgrath, Alister E. *Christian Theology: An Introduction*. Malden, MA: Blackwell, 2001.

McReynolds, Paul R. *Word Study: Greek-English*. Carol Stream: Tyndale House Publishers, 1999.

Melick, Richard R. *The New American Commentary: Philippians, Colossians, Philemon, electronic ed., Logos Library System.* Nashville: Broadman & Holman Publishers, 2001.

Microsoft. *Encarta ® World English Dictionary.* Redmond: Microsoft Corporation, 1998-2010.

Mirriam-Webster, Inc. *Mirriam-Webster's Collegiate Dictionary. Eleventh Edition.* Springfield: Mirriam-Webster, Inc., 2003.

Mounce, Robert H. *The New American Commentary: Vol. 27 Romans.* Nashville, TN: Broadman & Holman Publishers, 2001.

Mounce, William D. *Mounce's Complete Expository Dictionary of Old & New Testament Words.* Grand Rapids, MI: Zondervan, 2006.

Polhill, John B. *The New American Commentary 26: Acts.* Nashville: Broadman & Holman Publishers, 2001.

Pratt Jr, Richard L. *Holman New Testament Commentary: I & II Corinthians, vol. 7.* Nashville: Broadman & Holman Publishers, 2000.

Richardson, Kurt. *The New American Commentary Vol. 36 James.* Nashville: Broadman & Holman Publishers, 1997.

Robertson, A.T. *Word Pictures in the New Testament.* Oak Harbor, MI: Logos Research Systems, 1933, 1997.

Rooker, Mark F. *Leviticus: The New American Commentary.* Nashville: Broadman & Holman, 2001.

Ryrie, Charles C. *Basic Theology.* Chicago, IL: Moody Press, 1999.

Sweeney, Z. T. *The Spirit and the Word (: , n.d.), 121–26.* Nashville: Gospel Advocate, 2005.

Swindoll, Charles R, and Roy B. Zuck. *Understanding Christian Theology.* Nashville, TN: Thomas Nelson Publishers, 2003.

Towns, Elmer L. *Theology for Today.* Belmont: Wadsworth Group, 2002.

Vine, W E. *Vine's Expository Dictionary of Old and New Testament Words.* Nashville: Thomas Nelson, 1996.

Walls, David, and Max Anders. *Holan New Testament Commentary I & II Peter, I, II*

& III John, Jude. Nashville: Broadman & Holman Publishers, 1999.

Weber, Stuart K. *Holman New Testament Commentary, vol. 1, Matthew.* Nashville, TN: Broadman & Holman Publishers, 2000.

Wuest, Kenneth S. *Wuest's Word Studies from the Greek New Testament: For the English Reader.* Grand Rapids: Eerdmans, 1997, c1984.

Zodhiates, Spiros. *The Complete Word Study Dictionary: New Testament.* Chattanooga: AMG Publishers, 2000, c1992, c1993.